S.S. EDMUND FITZGERALD
REQUIEM FOR THE TOLEDO EXPRESS
A SEARCH FOR TRUTH

A Companion Account To The Author's Publication
For Whom The Bells Toll
by
Raymond Ramsay, M.Sc.

KEWEENAW MEDIA PRESS

Copyright© 2009 by Raymond Ramsay M.Sc.

All Rights Reserved. Except as permitted under the U.S. Copyright Act of 1976, no part of this book may be reproduced or transmitted in any form or by any means, electronic or mechanical, including photocopying, recording, or by any information storage and retrieval system without permission in writing from the publisher.

KEWEENAW MEDIA PRESS
P.O. Box 665
Houghton, Michigan 49931

Visit our website at www.keweenawmediapress.com

Printed in the United States of America

Library Of Congress Cataloging-in-Publication Data
Ramsay, Raymond
S.S. Edmund Fitzgerald Requiem For The "Toledo Express"
ISBN 13: 987-0-9791117-9-X
Price: $17.99 USD

First Printing May 2009

Author, Raymond Ramsay is responsible for all content in the publication
S.S. Edmund Fitzgerald – Requiem for the "Toldeo Express"

Managing Editor: Don Hermanson www.donhermanson.com
Book Design/Layout: B.J. Litsenberger www.theprintshophoughton.com
Copy Transcription: Wendy Wiegert www.thenatureofthings.ecrater.com
Cover Illustration: Kevin Breyfogle www.kevinbreyfogleart.ecrater.com
Cover Design: Jess Wiinamaki

For information or to order additional copies of:
Requiem For The Toledo Express
please write:
KEWEENAW MEDIA PRESS
P.O. Box 665
Houghton, MI. 49931
www.keweenawmediapress.com

With Dedication...

to the Great Lakes mariners who bravely voyaged on the S.S. Edmund Fitzgerald before her tragic sinking on November 10th 1975 without survivors, and the bereaved families who never received sound explanation, understanding or closure for the losses of their loved ones...

Record of Missing Crewmen of the S.S. Edmund Fitzgerald

Ernest M. McSorley, Master
John H. McCarthy, Chief Mate
James A. Pratt, Second Mate
George J. Holl, Chief Engineer
Michael E. Armagost, Third Mate
Edward F. Bindon, First Assistant Engineer
Thomas E. Edwards, Second Assistant Engineer
Russell G. Haskell, Second Assistant Engineer
Oliver J. Champeau, Third Assistant Engineer
Frederick J. Beetcher, Porter
Thomas Bentsen, Oiler
Thomas D. Borgeson, AB Maintenance Man
Nolan F. Church, Porter
Ranson E. Cundy, Watchman
Bruce L. Hudson, Deckhand

Allen G. Kalmon, Second Cook
Gordon F. MacLellan, Wiper
Joseph W. Mazes, Special Maintenance Man
Eugene W. O'Brien, Wheelsman
Karl A. Peckol, Watchman
John J. Poviach, Wheelsman
Robert C. Rafferty, Temporary Steward First Cook
Paul M. Riipa, Deckhand
John D. Simmons, Wheelsman
William J. Spengler, Watchman
Mark A. Thomas, Deckhand
Ralph G. Walton, Oiler
David E. Weiss, Cadet (deck)
Blaine H. Wilhelm, Oiler

With Grateful Acknowledgment...

for the generous pro-bono publico research contributed by dedicated supporters of the Casualty Research Associates in their search for maritime truth. The Associates represent a volunteer group of retired senior citizens having comprehensive technical credentials in the maritime field and professional association with the S.S. Edmund Fitzgerald design, construction and operation.

"Never doubt that a small group of thoughtful, committed citizens can change our world. Indeed it is the only thing that ever has."
- Margaret Mead, Anthropologist

AUTHOR'S BACKGROUND

Raymond Ramsay was educated and trained in England and now resides in Maryland, where he lives with his wife, Virginia and two children.

After a long career in merchant and naval vessel engineering and logistics management in both the private and government sectors, Mr. Ramsay retired from the Department of Defense (U.S. Navy) as the Director of the Office of Maritime Affairs and Shipbuilding Technology.

The Author, Raymond Ramsay M.Sc. and Hull # 301 S.S. Edmund Fitzgerald Great Lakes Engineering Works, River Rouge, Michigan, prior to launch June 1958

Image from Author's Collection

Launch day, June 7th, 1958

It was a beautiful Saturday afternoon as more than 10,000 peoople lined the banks of the Detroit River. They had come to witness the launching of Hull 301 at the Great Lakes Engineering Works of River Rouge, Michigan.

Image from Author's Collection

The Launch, June 7, 1958

Mrs. Edmund Fitzgerald, wife of the president of the Northwestern Mutual Life Insurance Company for which the ship was named, christened the brand new ship and at 12:34 p.m. the 729 ft. "Edmund Fitzgerald" slid gracefully into the basin amid cheers, salutes, and well wishers.

Image Courtesy of Dossin Great Lakes Museum Archives

Also by **RAYMOND RAMSAY, M.Sc.**

For Whom the Bells Toll:
The Unexplained Losses of S.S. Edmund Fitzgerald, M.V. Derbyshire, and Other Vessels of the Bulk-Cargo Silent Service
is a revealing and detailed study of the factors that may have contributed to tragic sinkings that occurred without evidence of a distress signal nor the presence of survivors or witnesses.

While focusing on the November 1975 loss of the S.S. Edmund Fitzgerald in the waters of Lake Superior, the Author also provides a descriptive background of inland marine commerce, drawing on his extensive personal and professional experience to develop reader understanding of the complex forces that have shaped the industry. He further considers similar occurrences and damages sustained on vessels of related design, drawing together a vast field of research to argue for the enhancement of safety and design standards.

For Whom the Bells Toll and Requiem for the Toledo Express convey the authors deep respect and concern for the mariners who serve in treacherous conditions around the world, and his careful consideration of the circumstances surrounding the losses serve as a just and well-reasoned call for reform.

Edition: Paperback • Price: $19.00
ISBN-13: 978-0-8099-6914-6 • ISBN-10: 0-8059-6914-4

For information or to order additional books please write:
Raymond Ramsay
13924 Blair Stone Lane
Silver Spring, MD 20906-3114

PREFACE

Over the past three years, since publication of the book "For Whom The Bells Toll" having dedication to Great Lakes and deep sea mariners who voyage in harm's way and their beloved aggrieved families, the Author chose to develop a companion edition entitled "Requiem For The Toledo Express". A rendition that gives specific recognition to the S. S. Edmund Fitzgerald vessel, with her highly capable officers and crew members, who continually made down-bound, high speed voyages from lakehead ore loading docks to feed the voracious appetites of steel mills in the downriver industrial area. This companion book presents a new review of hitherto unspoken circumstances that could have contributed to her demise and that of other vessels.

While it was the primary intent of the original book to appeal to technically-orientated students, historians, and those having interests in the high level bulk-cargo carrier losses on the Great Lakes and high seas, it was also intended to provide a measure of insight as to why so many losses occurred without warning, survivors, Mayday signals, witnesses or satisfactory public hearings…as necessary to ensure justice and appropriate monetary compensation for surviving families. The books were also researched to provide increased respect for highly-destructive environmental conditions affecting Great Lakes operations, and a global perspective regarding oceangoing bulk-cargo carrier casualty statistics.

In the 1990's, bulk-cargo vessels represented about 7% of oceangoing fleets, and they disproportionately sustained about 57% of the casualties. The average bulker loss rate from *unexplained circumstances* averaged about one per year.

In the case of Great Lakes vessels, over 6,000 vessels of lesser size than the S. S. Edmund Fitzgerald, are estimated to have been lost with one-third (1/3) due to *foundering* and with over one-half (1/2) of all *strandings* consistently occurring in the hazardous month of November... with considerable loss of mariner's lives.

Whether these be in recent or distant time frames, the probable causes for most vessel losses remain elusive when occurring without witnesses, survivors or distress signals and without benefit of adequate navigation equipment and reliable hydrographic information.

During public hearings, it was determined that the S. S. Edmund Fitzgerald could have been using chart Nos. L.S. 9 and vintage (1916), (1919) Canadian Chart 2310. They were confirmed by a CSS Bayfield hydrographic survey to be inaccurate...by failing to show that the northern end of the shoals North of Caribou Island extended approximately one mile further out into Lake Superior than indicated on the Canadian chart No. 2310!

This localized area re-survey appeared to be a shoaling "minefield" of navigational uncertainties, which were either used or avoided by experienced mariners who were able to recognize the "steepening" of wave heights and their frequency of wave encounter and bow slamming...when "smelling the land." In an overview, it is highly probable that hydrographers of a previous era had budget-constrained surveying priorities, at a time when earlier vessel drafts were of lesser risk to shoaling.

Consequently this could have negated a predisposition toward the exercise of a broader work scope, with regard to updating hydrographic information of the whole Canadian shoreline lee, from Thunder Bay to Sault Ste. Marie. Albeit shoaling risks would have still been present in the absence of modern navigational and communication equipment.

It may be fairly hypothesized that this whole hydrographic zone would most probably have had extensive shallower shoaling outcroppings (and shipwrecks) in the Canadian land mass littoral, which would have historically been contributory to an extensive graveyard of trading vessel casualties (of lesser design than Fitzgerald, and perhaps Fitzgerald herself) that may have encountered unmarked submerged obstructions.

While the CSS Bayfield's re-surveying operation successfully confirmed the Caribou Island and Superior Shoal topographic and geographic extent, it certainly did-not/could-not eliminate shoaling conjecture and the inconsistent evidence rendered by Fitzgerald's tracking observers on the S. S. Arthur M. Anderson Laker. (and others)

Regrettably, past and present writers and investigators have continued to concentrate on scenarios of perceived shoaling hazards off Caribou Island and to the detriment of some other candidate locations. All of which had technical dependency on vintage (circa 1919) hydrographic survey charts, which were only (in part) resurveyed as part of the USCG's Fitzgerald casualty investigation having bias toward mariner negligence, gradual hatch seal leakage and fatal hull damage due to shoaling.

From a deja-vu retrospective point of view, losses of two new (145 feet x 630 ton) French Navy minesweepers in 1918, en route from a Fort William, Ontario shipbuilder, are worthy of recall and may serve in a cautionary role, relative to a Fitzgerald penchant for misplaced conjectural events. Some historians have supported a likelihood that the "Cerisoles" and "Inkerman" grounded on Superior Shoal before sinking with the loss of 38 lives. (This shoal was not discovered by H.L. Leadman until the 1930's !) The unfounded position was taken, even though the official record was noncommittal by stating "The vessels probably foundered in a storm (on November 24th 1918)", although NO evidence was found. Later speculation was that they struck Superior Shoal. A pinnacle in the center of Lake Superior that was uncharted until the 1940's." Certainly reflecting "Positive Maybe" speculations.

In the Great Lakes operating theater, the prevailing technical standards and their implementation and regulation are openly called into question in support of viable conclusions that the S. S. Edmund Fitzgerald was determined to be:

> (a) Initially of advanced, structurally-austere design as driven by technological shortfalls, compliance with extrapolated longitudinal strength estimations (about 50% oceangoing standard), and acquisition cost limitations as a function of thriftiness and tech-

nical expediency. (Similar deficiencies were reflected in almost-sister "Arthur B. Homer" of Bethlehem Steel, after high-expenditure lengthening before early layup and dismantling).

(b) Fabricated with flawed weld deposition and quality control, as demonstrable by defective (and "slugged") weld joints, and steel plating critical to hull structural integrity. Almost all-welded hull construction was pioneered during the high-production years of World War II shipbuilding, and similarly required repetitive weld repairs. Deferrals of critical welding repairs shortened service life and contributed to many losses.

(c) Additionally overstressed by overloading (about 4,000 tons) to deeper drafts as permitted by the (1969-1973) Load Line Amendment, and authorized by the United States Coast Guard (USCG), with technical support from the American Bureau of Shipping (ABS)...*without* retrofit design or installation of hull structural reinforcement.

(d) Significantly damaged by collisions with S.S. Hochelaga, dock walls and groundings requiring steel patches and welding repairs in outer shell plating, and difficult to inspect critical internal structure over a five-year period.

(e) Life-cycle maintenance and repair deferrals to conserve expense and maintain schedules.

(f) Perceived conflicts of professional interest by regulatory (USCG) and private sector representatives...(Especially when post-retirement "revolving doors" were opened for employment opportunities).

The Fitzgerald was chartered to Columbia Transportation Division of the Oglebay Norton Company and was not owned by a steel-producing Corporation. With such business Genesis, investor expenditures for Fitzgerald's acquisition, and operation were rigidly controlled and there were expectations of high cargo-hauling performance.

Hence, the exemplary achievements of Captains Pulcer, and McSorley who may have been further incentivized by tonnage bonus provisions...and/or command relief if incurring delays or non-availability for service. In Fitzgerald's final days, it is highly probable that Captain McSorley knew of the high-risk nature of the hull structural degradation due to inadequate repair and maintenance.

A number of theories have been advanced by technical and non-technical parties to explain the loss of S.S. Edmund Fitzgerald, and some have expressed difficulty with the "complexity" of my book's rationale which has dependency on naval architectural principles and empirical history of ship structures...albeit human and business considerations were not disregarded.

The Author applied both esoteric (1950's) naval architectural and generic structural mechanics principles to estimate stresses and flexibility of the semi-monocoque Laker hull structure appropriate to that point in time.

The following companion book seeks to build on "For Whom The Bells Toll" by pulling back a veil to provide a measure of public exposure, to unspoken facts about the application of over-extrapolated design criteria resulting in shortened service life, excessive structural bending, springing, twisting and the metal fatigue failure of steel plating and its welding.

Considerable data was collected by interpersonal contact with technical, production, regulatory, and mariner personnel having first-hand experience within their fields of expertise, and having professional concern about the communication "cover-up" associated with the Fitzgerald birth, life, and passing.

There is no iconoclastic motivation involved in writing either book, although some may (again) ask the question "Why did it take thirty years to come forward."

The Author's answer is that retirement time availability, reasonably complete records, and a sound mind have made it possible to make disclosures to the best of my ability to assist aggrieved family members who may seek to reopen inquiries pursuant to the Rule of Law within the U.S. Judiciary.

Her last load out, November 9th, 1975 - Superior Wisconsin Entry
Image Courtesy of Artist Doris Sampson

Captain Ernest M. McSorley
Image Courtesy of Great Lakes
Shipwreck Historical Society

The following Benjamin Franklin Quotation Appears To Have Relevance
When Timely Maintenance And Repair Are Vital Issues:

"For want of a Horseshoe Nail the Shoe was lost; for want of a Shoe the Horse was lost; and for the want of a Horse the Rider was lost; being overtaken by the enemy and the battle lost... and all for want of a Nail."

A STAR WAS BORN

The birth of the *S.S. Edmund Fitzgerald* was marked by her keel laying on August 7th 1957 at the Great Lakes Engineering Works shipyard in River Rouge, Michigan. The newborn was destined to become a short-lived shining star within a galaxy of other Laker vessels that carry the lifeblood of our national economy, while toiling within the geographically-restricted and weather-sensitive Great Lakes region.

The growing-up and adult years of Fitzgerald were expected to abide by the "house rules" under legislated provisions of the Jones Act that mandates American ownership, crewing, domestic shipyard design, construction and (USCG) regulation augmented by the American Bureau of Shipping (ABS) Classification Society's technical expertise.

> *Within such a protective envelope the "Big Fitz's" foster parents became obligated to fully meet maintenance and repair commitments. They were also obligated to follow good business practices while nurturing careful operations necessary to preserve a safe condition of vital interest to crew members, the owners and operators, and to ensure the annual award of a regulatory Certificate of Inspection...without which she could not ply Great Lakes waters to earn a living.*

The Star's performance continued to shine brightly to the world at large, albeit physiological (structural) weaknesses were suspected in her prebirth genetic makeup, as was the questionable satisfaction of maintenance and repair commitments during her short lifetime and before her catastrophic demise.

The author's prior book "For Whom The Bells Toll" was written for the purpose of facilitating Laker and oceangoing bulk-cargo vessel design and construction insight, and to bring awareness to vulnerability from unique genetic weaknesses, based on casualty statistics.

This book "Requiem for the Toledo Express" is a companion account based on privileged interviews and research readings, as another "footprint in the snow" conducive to developing broadened understanding of Fitzgerald's loss.

- Raymond Ramsay -

Columbia Transportation Division
Charterer of Oglebay Norton Company

S.S. Edmund Fitzgerald
Image Courtesy of Great Lakes
Shipwreck Historical Society

L. Length B.P./LOA . . . . 711/729 ft.
B. Breadth 75
D. Depth 39
L/D Ratio 18.2
F. Freeboard 11.5
Displacement . . . . 35,000 tons
Block Coefficient 0.88
Cargo Deadweight . . . . 26,116 tons
Cargo Hold Capacity . . . . 860,950 cub. ft.
V. Speed . . . . 14.15 knots (16.30 mph)
V/L Speed-Length Ratio 0.53
Loss Of Lives 29

SHINING A LIGHT ON HIDDEN TRUTHS

In the recent past the author does recall that President George Walker Bush spoke of a "Thousand Points Of Light" to further the progress of our great country. The interpretation of his intent was that the generation of such light should come from our able citizenry, and mainly through daily contributions in thought, word and deed to our society...and most notably in the form of volunteerism.

Many of us have responded and experienced success or failure, together with criticism having either justified or unjustified bases. In the latter case, some unwarranted criticism has been based on rumor filling a vacuous state of disinformation and a general lack of appreciation regarding motivational goals...especially when directed at our volunteer group known as Casualty Research Associates (CRA). We are composed of senior citizens having comprehensive technical credentials and experience in the maritime field and, as retirees of sound mind, we have freedom of thought and action unrestricted by management constraints affecting income and tenure.

While one of our initial goals was to develop an objective three-part "cradle-to-the-grave" historical documentary covering the development, construction and operation of S.S. Edmund Fitzgerald, investigatory efforts have experienced considerable difficulty for reasons not fully expressed by knowledgeable persons ranging from the shipyard tradesman to executive and Government regulatory levels. (i.e. "Gag" orders prevalent).

Based on these circumstances, our original investigatory scope has been expanded to encompass "We don't know what we didn't know" avenues that have led to startling legerdemain discoveries in our self-motivated search for truth.

To whom it may concern:
We have no plans to extinguish our uncompensated volunteer "Point of Light" beacon that will continue to shine until unbiased truth, or justifiable termination cause, is forthcoming.
Thank you.

CONTENTS

	Author's Background	v
	Preface	ix
	A Star Was Born	xvi
	Shining a Light On Hidden Truths	xviii
1.0	Prologue	1
	Captain Peter P. Pulcer	2
	Load Line Regulation Amendment	3
	Captain Ernest M. McSorley	5
2.0	Lake Superior (Gitche Gumee) Victims	11
3.0	The Toledo Express	15
4.0	Public Hearing Outcomes	19
5.0	The Wiggly Thing	29
6.0	The Crux	35
7.0	A Reminiscent Soliloquy	44
7.1	Prefabrication And Welding	45
7.2	Shipyard Environment	47
8.0	Comparisons And Contrasts	57
8.1	Shipyards and Practices	57
8.2	Design Considerations	58
8.3	Design Premising	62
9.0	The 1930's Commission	67
10.0	Needed Structural Modifications	70
10.1	Increased Cargo Loading	74
10.2	Need for Cargo Hatch Cover And Coaming Strengthening	75
11.0	Hindsight Perspectives	83
11.1	Public Hearing Dilemmas	83
11.2	Cargo Loading And Transportation	87
11.3	Potential (Other) Shipments (National Security	89
11.4	Potential (Other) Shipments (Higher Value Minerals)	91
11.5	S.S. Carl D. Bradley Loss Comparison	92
12.0	Hull Destruction Dioramas	94
13.0	Shoaling (or not)	99
14.0	Storm Effects (Seiche-Surge-Clapotis)	104
15.0	Circumstantial Propositions (Lemmas 1 through 13)	111
16.0	Cargo Hold Flooding	120
17.0	Epilogue	122
17.1	Toward Justice And Kinder Times	129
17.2	Summation	132
18.0	References And Resources	141
	Appendix I, S.S. Carl D. Bradley Claims	144
	Appendix II, S.S. Edmund Fitzgerald Petition	145
	Appendix III, Congressional Hearing May 19 2008	146

Image from Author's collection

- 1.0 -
PROLOGUE

With every passing year many maritime devotees, including myself, continue to feel strong ties to the first and fastest St. Lawrence Seaway-sized Laker to enter Great Lakes service after her September 1958 delivery from the Great lakes Engineering Works (GLEW) shipyard in River Rouge, Michigan.

It is over thirty-three years since the S. S. Edmund Fitzgerald disappeared from our Great Lakes fleet, and many volumes of written appraisal, mainly centered on perceived (commercially-profitable) mystique and supposition, have been generated by experts and novices alike.

And, over the past three years, significant factual data have been discovered and analyzed by Casualty Research Associates (CRA) in their search for truth with indisputable cause and effect evidence for her loss.

The following presentation is an abbreviated and well-documented expose adhering to a discovery philosophy that "When a researcher/presenter does not have substantiated facts he is restricted to pounding on the table, and when statements and credible eye-witnesses and/or bona-fide historic supporting evidence are discovered, then there are firm grounds for believability and determinations of culpability."

To this end, certain multi-talented and dedicated professionals have labored on an unbiased pro bono publico basis to establish credibility and the necessary factual evidence to support their findings which are outlined herein.

In our search for unbiased truths we unfortunately found it necessary to include a melancholy "Requiem" term in the article title. This was primarily done in an effort to dedicate a religious hymn or dirge for survivor families and the repose of their dead...and not to grieve for corporate losses.

Image Courtesy of Great Lakes Shipwreck Historical Society

CAPTAIN PETER P. PULCER

As a mea culpa, we do fully realize that such a choice does severely contrast with the late Captain Peter P. Pulcer's stereo-amplified and exhilarating "hillbilly" and classical music selections, his pilot house exterior floral displays, and his running commentaries in halcyon times when in command (1966-1971) of the record-setting vessel.

He was indeed an enthusiastic and cautious Master of the then-deservedly named "Pride of the American Flag" as a record-holder for hauling iron ore. The USCG Load Line Amendment (1969-1973) authorized reductions in assigned freeboard...that allowed deeper seasonal drafts commensurate with prevailing water depths and the facilitation of increases in cargo-carrying capacity.

USCG Load Line Regulation Amendment

Between 1958 and 1973, the Fitzgerald was permitted three reductions in the minimum freeboard required by 46 CFR Part 45. (Freeboard on the Fitzgerald was the distance from the maximum draft permitted to

Minimum Required Freeboard

Date	Midsummer	Summer	Intermediate	Winter
Originally assigned when vessel was built	11 feet-10 3/4 inch	12 feet-6 3/4 inch	13 feet-6 3/4 inch	14 feet-9 1/4 inch
3 July 69	11 feet-4 1/2 inch	12 feet-1/2 inch	13 feet-3/4 inch	14 feet-3 1/2 inch
17 Sept 71	11 feet-4 1/2 inch	12 feet-1/2 inch	13 feet-3/4 inch	13 feet-2 inch
13 Sept 73	10 feet-5 1/2 inch	11 feet-2 inch	11 feet-2 inch	**11 feet-6 inch****

46 CFR 45.5 states that midsummer freeboard applied May 1 through September 15; summer freeboard applied April 16 through April 30 and September 16 through September 30; intermediate freeboard applied October 1 through October 31 and April 1 through April 15; and <u>winter</u> freeboard applies November 1 through March 31.

****Thus, the deepest Winter load line applied to Fitzgerald at the time of her last loading.**

3

the spar deck at side.) A comparison of the requirements for Great Lakes cargo vessels and those for vessels operating on the oceans shows that for vessels of similar dimensions, the freeboard required for a Great lakes Load Line and that required for ocean service would be approximately the same. However, the longitudinal strength required for a Great lakes vessel is approximately 1/2 of that required for a vessel in ocean service. The foregoing table shows the freeboards assigned to the Fitzgerald.

It was estimated that the deeper-draft Winter loading enabled an additional 4,000 tons of cargo to be transported per trip. This was about 15% above the original deadweight on which the initial (extrapolated) structural design criteria were based.

No known hull reinforcement designs or installations were made to accommodate the additional *Winter* loading condition which could have had negative influence on the vessel's handling, pronounced hull flexibility, and lifetime durability.

However, the late Captain Pulcer is understood to have been resistant to business pressures when he declined to take full advantage of the Fitzgerald's expanded ore-cargo hauling capability for further enhancement of his pace- setting achievements.

It is highly probable that, after five years of Fitzgerald's command, he must have been well aware of:

> (1) The attritional shipboard wear and tear effects of deeper draft loading <u>without</u> appropriate hull structural reinforcement, and full knowledge of his vessel's dubious material condition toward the end of her service life, when the amplitudes and frequencies of hull bending, springing and torsional flexibilities were becoming of increased concern, *and*
>
> (2) The negative hydrodynamic immersion effects on ship handling response caused by increases in loaded draft and the additional underwater wetted surface drag <u>*without*</u> any modification of rudder area and steering system characteristics.

There were reports of "sluggishness" in handling response during authorized deeper-draft operation, even though the original rudder was of streamlined design with about 20% balance forward of the rudder stock, and a maximum rudder angle of 45 degrees which could be achieved with a hardover to hardover time of 20 seconds.

To his credit and intuitive mariner know-how, he may have also recognized the compound stress-inducing and abnormal multi-axial flexibilities of the hull structure which he would have chosen not to further compromise.

In retrospect, the questioning Watergate words of Senator Howard Baker (R-Tenn) of "What did he and owner-investors know, (about the Fitzgerald's condition) and when did they know it??" could have been deserving of repetition.

Image Courtesy of Great Lakes
Shipwreck Historical Society

CAPTAIN ERNEST M. McSORLEY

The latter situation may have also become evident to his successor Captain Ernest M. McSorley (1972-1975) who was also under pressure and had a fleet-wide reputation as a demanding ship driver and a safe all-weather mariner, who could claim shipfitting experience in his early career.

This Great Lakes veteran master had been employed by the Fitzgerald's operator since 1938; where he was a ship master since 1951; and had served as master of the Fitzgerald since April 1972.

It is ironic that this Canadian-born mariner, who came to America when he was eleven (11) years old, should spend a lifetime in Great Lakes service and would eventually be returned to Canadian soil upon his death after the Fitzgerald catastrophe terminated his career...He was once the youngest master of a Laker, and was on his final scheduled (1975) voyage with planned retirement in mind for the following year.

In a final analysis these factors cannot be disregarded by critics, even though certain crew members are known to have had ad-hoc opinions of laissez-faire or authoritarian command management practices by various vessel masters.

In carrying out his duties, Captain McSorley's psyche left no doubt that he was an experienced and committed "company man" by his very actions and when vocally expressing his work ethic that "Can't make no money setting at anchor, laying at anchor." (At another point in Americana transportation history, he could have been compared with Casey Jones who drove legendary Locomotive 382 to destruction in a high-speed crash *through no fault of his own*...and left behind a grieving wife with three children).

In keeping with his cost-conscious work ethic, Captain McSorley was also predictable in reallocating shipboard work to shipyard accomplishment, rather than have contractors work on board and possibly incur voyage delays.

He was also expected to deny weekend overtime payment for the cleanup of taconite pellets strewn on the exposed spar deck even though it was a union general rule that, if a vessel left after midnight, a cleared walkway was required on one side or the other, depending on weather conditions.

It was usually the lee side, unless loading on the other (starboard) side was in progress, and where deck space was usually strewn with taconite pellets, dirt, or other detritus.

Rather than pay overtime to keep the spar deck clear over the weekend, Captain McSorley would exercise his management judgment and control prerogatives, when allowing crew members to safely use the two under- deck tunnels until the spar deck was made shipshape and "Bristol Fashion," after cleanup was recommenced on Monday morning.

While neither master would profess to being stress analyst technocrats or behaviorists specializing in human engineering, their continuously dedicated Laker service would have certainly generated a symbiotic (gut feel) understanding of their highly-responsible man-machine interface.

Like many other migrant "foreigners," who were later caught up in a professional "Brain Drain," the Author had early attraction to the uniquely pristine Great Lakes region. And, during World War II schooldays in England as a potential evacuee, he could not possibly have envisioned future familial and professional ties to River Rouge, which he originally thought was on the Canadian mainland near Windsor, Ontario!!

This geographic location was where the Author met his wife (1958) and commenced his first maritime employment in the United States with the Great Lakes Engineering Works (GLEW) shipyard...which was under contract to deliver three very-similar straight-decker Laker vessels.

Winter Lay-Up, 1964-1965 - Fraser Shipyard, Duluth Harbor
Image Courtesy of Wes Harkin, Fraswer Ship Yard

Image Courtesy of Canal Park Maritime Museum, Duluth, Minnesota

S.S. Edmund Fitzgerald (Hull No. 301)

Based on 20/20 hindsight and developing Laker awareness, it is indeed fortuitous that the shipowner did not proceed with design proposals (1966) that considered post-delivery options for lengthening her bending, springing and twisting hull by up to 144 feet.

Photo by Kenneth Newhams, Duluth Shipping News

S.S. Herbert C. Jackson (Hull No. 302)

Was not lengthened, but was subsequently converted to a self-unloader in the late 1970's and is still in service under less strenuous operation than Fitzgerald.

S.S. Arthur B. Homer (Hull No. 303)

Subsequently was lengthened by 96 feet at the Fraser shipyard (1976), and afterwards exhibited increased hull flexure even though additional hull reinforcement was incorporated.

In 1972 the "Homer" sustained underway collision damage with Greek "saltie" Navshipper, which did not have licensed pilotage. The "Homer" was later laid-up in 1980 by the Bethlehem Steel Corporation shipowners, before dismantling in 1987.

With the passage of time and benefiting from sound-mind retirement, the Author continues to feel strong naval architectural and humanitarian interest in the Fitzgerald, her crew, survivor families and improved standards,...albeit without personal financial or aggrandizement gain motivation.

S.S. Arthur B. Homer (left) and the Navshipper (right)
The S.S. Arthur B. Homer, loaded with iron ore, was in a head-on collision on October 5 1972. There were no injuries, but the Homer suffered extensive bow damage up to and including part of her pilothouse.
Image Courtesy of Great Lakes Shipwreck Historical Society

The primary interest is a search for truth, with others having like interests and clear passage through over thirty years of obfuscation, engendered by self-serving factions who felt bound by historical technical precedents, and showed little or no regard for the humanities associated with lost mariners and their surviving family members.

Based on the newly-accumulated evidence, CRA does *not* subscribe to the "Mystery and Mystique" mantra which has surrounded the S.S. Edmund Fitzgerald for over thirty (30) years. Faith is placed in factual information that has "beyond reasonable doubt" credibility.

The Fitzgerald loss is but one of many known vessel casualty situations having a long history of Great Lakes and global mariner neglect. They have never been fully addressed within judicial systems and justice is considered to be long overdue.

- 2.0 -
LAKE SUPERIOR (GITCHE GUMEE) VICTIMS

While Fitzgerald's seventeen-year (1958-1975) operational life was considerably shorter than that for many older and smaller-sized Lakers having significantly less speed and propulsion power, she was able to establish an ore-carrying leadership reputation before catastrophically breaking-up under severe storm conditions, and sinking to a water depth of 530 feet approximately seventeen miles from safe haven at Whitefish Bay, Michigan on November 10th 1975.

Before her demise, on the 40th voyage of her 17th season, The Fitzgerald's pace-setting performance and sound public relations made her deserving of "Pride of the American Flag" recognition, although design limitations and hull construction deficiencies would eventually become exposed and receive increased scrutiny toward the end of her exhaustive lifetime. (Her final resting place is partly in Canadian waters protected by the Ontario Heritage Act licensing requirements for general surveys and the collection of research data).

All of the vessel's twenty-nine officers and crew members were reported as missing and presumed dead. No distress signals or eyewitnesses were reported.

From the Record, the Fitzgerald's Certificate of Inspection dated April 9th 1975 shows registry for forty-nine (49) (versus 29) persons, and there are no data to determine the actual number of persons on board at the time of sinking on November 10th 1975...or official requirement for such complement.

May they rest in peace with fellow Great Lakes mariners from an estimated 6,000 lost ships, with less than half of their hulls located. Statistically, between the years 1900 and 1950, it was estimated that one-third were lost due to *foundering*, and with over one-half of all *strandings* simultaneously occurring in the hazardous month of November...with

S.S. Edmund Fitzgerald
Photo by Robert Cambell, courtesy of University of Wisconsin - Superior

considerable loss of mariners' lives. (Ref: "Shipwrecks of the Great Lakes"- Dana T. Bowen.)

The Author is averse to the attribution of these casualties to cause majeure (Acts of God) forces alone, and prefers to fault vessel design criteria founded on (1950's) traditional heuristic reasoning and Classification Society (American Bureau of Shipping, Lloyd's Register et al) extrapolations of empirical bases... having a paucity of Research, Development, Testing and Evaluation (RDT&E) foundation, coupled with questionable production and fabricated material quality control procedures.

In more recent times, a number of Great Lakes families have mourned the losses of their loved ones who served on the following vessels:

        S.S. Henry Steinbrenner . . . .May 11 1953 . . . . . . .17 deaths
        S.S. Carl D. Bradley . . . . . . .Nov. 18 1958 . . . . . . .33 deaths
        S.S. Cedarville . . . . .May 7 1965 . . . . .10 deaths
        S.S. Daniel J. Morrell . . . . . .Nov. 29 1966 . . . . . . .28 deaths
        S.S. Edmund Fitzgerald . . . .Nov. 10 1975 . . . . . . .29 deaths

Contributory causes for the losses have included such considerations as heavy weather, cargo-load and/or ballast water amount and distribution, repair deferrals and maintenance expense avoidance (neglect), human error, and a vessel's development time frame relative to the naval architectural design and construction technologies of each shipbuilding era. These causes are exclusive of a USCG Marine Board penchant attaching blame to crew negligence and faulty weather tightening cargo hatch covers.

It is notable that the S.S. Edmund Fitzgerald had a shortened operational (17-year) lifespan with a 1950's design (optimistically) extrapolated from earlier Lakers... which, in hindsight was not a structural, parent family subjected to leading-edge Research, Development Testing and Evaluation (RDT&E) principles, whenever minimum guidance standards were found to be inadequate.

Later actions by the American Bureau Of Shipping (ABS) in the promulgation of 1978 Rules For Building and Classing Bulk Carriers on the Great Lakes were commendable, although application mainly benefited 1,000 foot + bulkers of different structural configuration (to Fitzgerald) and geographically confined to operations in the Upper Lakes...and having no commonality with the Fitzgerald structural concept, operational profiles, or contribution to an expost facto affirmative casualty analysis.

The Author does not share a viewpoint that the formulation and promulgation of these (1978) ABS Rules was fostered by an overt <u>admission</u> of Fitzgerald's structural design inadequacy (based on experience and heuristic reasoning). Although, there are some observers who do view the ABS et al initiative to revise structural criteria as an admission of Fitzgerald 1950's design deficiencies.

Rather, the ABS technical and economic challenges on 1,000 foot + bulkers would have been focused on cost-effective ramifications (i.e. following an expenditure and revenue dictum) with safe transportation of bulk-cargoes having at least <u>three</u> times the revenue-producing capability achievable by a Fitzgerald-sized vessel...and with additional precautions for all- weather operations.

Also, it is considered notable that none of the other Lakers (which were directly relatable to the Fitzgerald's design but operated within the same operator's fleet) suffered losses during the Fitzgerald's service time frame. This factor is considered to be supportive of prognoses that potentially inadequate design, construction, repair and maintenance were present in Fitzgerald and should have merited a higher level of consideration during post-sinking public hearings.

Further doubtful technical shadows should have also been cast when her almost sister Laker "S.S. Arthur B. Homer" demonstrated a similar severe pattern of hull-flexing characteristics, before and after an unsafe deadweight- enhancing cargo hold lengthening by ninety-six (96) feet was executed by Fraser Shipyard. Her resultant flexibility response proved to be unacceptable, even though structural reinforcement had been retrofitted before a long layup that preceded final dismantling.

With the conversion of the almost-sister Laker S.S. "Herbert C. Jackson" to a <u>self-unloader</u> her (stiffer) internally-modified structural arrangement could have reduced hull flexibility concerns inherited from Fitzgerald. In other words, the self-unloader conversion work made significant contribution to "dodging an extreme hull-flexibility generic bullet."

Nevertheless, even though the "Jackson's" hull conversion to a self-unloader also demonstrated positive structural benefit, in contrast to "Fitzgerald" and "Homer's" excessive flexibility while remaining as straight-deckers, it would (still) appear technically prudent for USCG Inspectors to order expost facto structural inspections, of known carryover areas having questionable workmanship and strength. (Structural carryover deficits may have originated during the "Jackson's" initial (1959) fabrication at the GLEW shipyard or were subsequently produced during in-service repairs, maintenance or regulatory USCG inspections).

- 3.0 -
THE TOLEDO EXPRESS

Great Lakes families and mariners were well acquainted with the Fitzgerald's legendary ore-carrying achievements, especially her routinely high-speed runs between the lake-head loading docks and downstream steel making plants near Toledo Ohio.

These direct "Toledo Express" transits allowed full advantage to be taken of the impressive Westinghouse Electric steam turbine propulsion plant having capability to deliver 7,500 shaft horsepower, with power reserve to provide a continuous maximum output of 8,200.

The vessel's high level of propulsion efficiency also benefited from

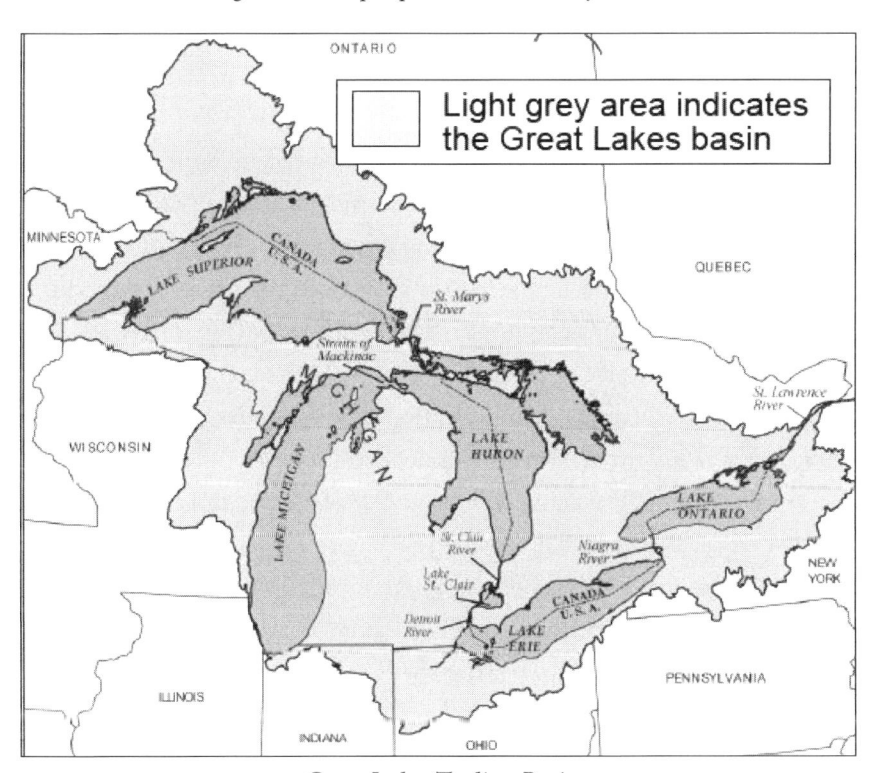

Great Lakes Trading Basin

expertly designed hydrodynamic qualities of the fine stern lines and incorporation of carefully selected propeller features. On the other hand, the unmatched propulsive thrust would have increased slamming of the "blunt" bow when encountering steep, frequent lake waveforces...moreso than lesser-powered and smaller vessels.

Needless to say, the Northwestern Mutual Life Insurance Company shipowners, their investors and Oglebay Norton Bare Boat charterer and their Columbia Transportation Division should have earned a very favorable financial return from the original eight-million (1958) dollar investment. Apart from charisma, the vessel was well-qualified as a "cash-cow" profit center in a known environment of maintenance and repair neglect.

To construct such a vessel over a 44-week (keel-laying to launching) period appeared to reflect good industrial planning, modular prefabrication, and execution...as did the ore-hauling performance records over an eleven- year period when about one million tons per year were regularly shipped through the Soo locks.

However, and in retrospect after the Fitzgerald sinking, a number of technical questions have been raised concerning welding during construction and for design and structural adequacy, cargo loading, and the soundness of repairs and life-cycle maintenance in the quest to seek closure for a wide number of factors considered contributory to the vessel's demise and crew member deaths. <u>The Author (and others) emphatically disagree that the Fitzgerald hull was physically in seaworthy condition prior to her final voyage.</u> (Ref. NTSB.Report) (Page 44)

Prior to the 1973 welding failures and 1974 Winter layup, the USCG determined that Fitzgerald had experienced various amounts of hull fatigue damage in the course of her working career, and hair-line steel-work cracking joining the steel hatch-end girders and the hatch-end coamings, had occurred beneath the spar deck plating.

Hatch openings had four (4) welded joints at each of the corner stress concentration locations and, of the eighty-four (84) joints total, twenty-four (24) were found with structural cracks. Fitzgerald was exhibiting welding failures, well-known to WWII mass-production when welding procedures, training, and stress predictions were not fully developed.

Some of the Fitzgerald's cracks were repaired during vessel layup periods, but the repairs were followed by cracking <u>repetition</u> as a function of weld failures and vessel springing, bending and torsional flexibility throughout the 1974-1975 operating season and some were/were-*not* subsequently re-welded to offset debilitating effects on hull structural integrity. In addition, at least 4,000 linear feet of ballast tank structural welding were "red-flagged" by the USCG 10 days prior to the final voyage,...but this repair work was deferred.

Regrettably, evidence reviews and search-for-truth inquiries by CRA, regarding the seriousness and scope completeness of the foregoing repair work were met by a paucity of open communication, that was further impeded by perceived conspiracies of (*gag order*) silence. Some of which were exhibited by organizations and their employees having vested interests, including but not limited to, their job security; liability compensation; and potential court litigation outcomes.

It became evident that many organizational elements, including official USCG vessel safety regulators, the Great Lakes shipping industry, et al., have perpetuated a cover-up ("A Strong Neutral Stand") to protect their "fiefdom turf" reputations, financial resources, and shipowner insurance actuaries with the following parameters in mind:

- <u>If a vessel is lost due to shipowner negligence to keep and maintain a safe vessel, then that shipowner is financially liable for most of the losses suffered.</u>
- If a vessel is lost for reasons other than the negligence of a shipowner, then that shipowner is only financially responsible for a vessel's value.
- A fairly common finding of fault on the part of the officers and crew (connoting a vessel's master) limits responsibility to a ship-owner and his insurers. Under such circumstances it is high-

ly probable that the shipowner-investors would keep a low profile when aware of the Fitzgerald's poorly maintained condition, while seeking deflection of negligence on the officers and crew.

These circumstances also include questionable "hands-off" diver restrictions requiring a Province of Ontario permit for accessing the Fitzgerald wreckage site, which is partly located in Canadian waters, and considered as a marine sanctuary.

Minimal informational dialogue has been experienced, but this may be partially attributable to strict enforcement of Canadian border security measures against global terrorism.

The reluctance of some parties, having first-hand knowledge of the Fitzgerald's material condition, would appear to have placed barriers to the USCG and shipowner release of maintenance and repair history information as necessary for safe Laker operation and inquiry. The situation also continues to be exacerbated by an abundance of conjecture and ineffectiveness in consequence of:

- There is a prevailing general public reluctance to accept official reports by the National Transportation Safety Board (NTSB) and the United States Coast Guard (USCG)Marine Board of Investigation that have <u>failed to achieve unanimity in the establishment of cause and effect decisional parameters.</u>
- The post-delivery deteriorated hull condition was well known to welders and technical consultants, who were confronted by hazardous non-workable access conditions, and shipyards, that declined to accept deteriorated Fitzgerald maintenance and repair work.

- 4.0 -
PUBLIC HEARING OUTCOMES

It is a strong personal view of the Author that the NTSB and USCG hearing panels' very limited official Findings of Fact scoping impeded technical closure, a full identification of liabilities, and an adequate rationale for awarding appropriate compensation for those parties directly harmed by this catastrophic event.

And, it would appear that liabilities of the Fitzgerald shipowner, government regulatory agencies, actuarial bodies et al, can only be removed from a limbo status (after 33 years) by resolving major issues according to the Rule of Law within the <u>United States judicial system.</u> As minimum:

(1) Did the Fitzgerald fail to survive after navigating incorrectly charted or uncharted shoal areas (Caribou Island or other)? *or*

(2) Did the Fitzgerald fail to survive storm conditions with structural failure, due to deferred or ineffective repair and maintenance prior to final voyage departure?

(3) Did the Fitzgerald fail to survive due to a combination of 1 and 2?

(4) Did the Fitzgerald hold a credible USCG Certificate of Inspection, (without restrictions) for safety and soundness?

(5) Was the Fitzgerald's log book retrieved during sanitation diving operations that cleaned the sunken pilothouse...and later had entries reconstructed from memory.

(6) What was the final cargo composition, distribution, and crew complement based on the sailing manifest record?

(7) Did the maintenance and calibration records show Fitzgerald and Anderson radar systems in a state of operational readiness?

The CRA research has made discoveries, since cessation of (1975) public Hearings, to provide <u>proof beyond a reasonable doubt</u> that inadequacies and the neglect of vessel maintenance and repair impaired

The Fitzgerald's pilot house
Images Courtesy of G.L.S.H.S.

the safety of Great Lakes mariners.

The Author considers that CRA's independent discoveries, have demonstrated that the presiding panel of public hearing members had very limited scope and approaches to establishing Findings of Fact, tantamount to a cover-up strategy for protection of their own professional career and organizational reputations. They appeared to be tradition-bound, and most-amenable to assigning probable cause to crew members and leaking (versus collapsing) hatch covers.

Although a single dissenting opinion was recorded, no proviso was forthcoming for future authorization to reopen the case, should further evidence be discovered.

There is now sufficient evidence at hand to apprise the Great Lakes maritime community that Fitzgerald's deteriorated hull condition should have been well known by shipowners and operators, and during regulatory inspection intervals over her rigorous lifetime,...The conditions should have been officially documented in government records prepared and requiring archival retention by the USCG regulatory authority.

After considerable objective survey by CRA, it would appear that the panelists failed to adequately research Fitzgerald's design, construction, maintenance and repair histories, within a limited preordered hearing scope envelope that had no bearing on a "A maritime casualty about to happen over a longer term."

This has occurred many times in the cases of "borderline bulk-cargo vessels classified by the American Bureau of Shipping (ABS) and others throughout the world.

For example, during the course of the 38-year old S.S. Mariner Electric" sinking investigations (of February 12th 1983), her self-serving shipowners theorized that the vessel ran aground in coastal waters off Virginia, and this caused the sinking five hours later... with the tragic loss of 31 out of 34 lives.

However, a review of USCG and other investigations revealed faked seaworthiness certification, by disregarding gaping holes in corroded deck plating and hatch covers, and the showing of fraudulent inspection ABS records for unseaworthy hatch covers that had been actually off-hull and unavailable for maintenance.

Herein lies a prevailing conflict of interest since vessel inspection fees are paid (to the ABS) by shipowners and in recent times, positive actions of the International Association of Classification (IACS) are reported to have been somewhat effective, subsequent to the British oceangoing M.V. Derbyshire (OBO) loss in 1980. It is claimed that their initiative has been instrumental in improving the safety of older bulk-cargo vessels on the international scene, by the arrest or slowing down of the rate of "total loss" claimants who were being paid as "can't lose" shipowners by insurance actuaries.

For example, in the 1980-1996 time frame, 43 ill-maintained aging vessels of over 200,000 tons deadweight, and their crews, were lost under oceangoing circumstances where structural failure could have played a part. During the years 1990-1991, losses occurred for 25 vessels of over 15,000 tons deadweight. As the Author stated in his book "For Whom The Bells Toll" (Re: pp 86- Exposure of Global Bulk Cargo Losses), these mounting vessel and mariner losses appeared to represent a very large skeleton in a very dark closet."

However, a remarkable improvement was recorded in 2005 when the (younger) average oceangoing bulker was just over 13 years old, with about 41% of all bulkers less than ten (10) years old. (FYI-On the Great Lakes, most of the (98) registered bulkers were in excess of twenty (20) years of age), and annually carried about 3.2 million tons of cargo...a minor proportion of the 1.7 billion tons in world trade bulk-cargo carriers.

While the cargo capacities and populations of oceangoing bulk-cargo vessels are rapidly-increasing in developing (Far-Eastern) countries having considerably-extended trading routes, it would appear that their fleets now include relatively-new mammoth bulkers, of 300,000 tons dwt.

Their "newness" and technological improvements in design, inspection and maintenance have no doubt made significant contribution to casualty reductions. However, one must guard against overbuilding and the sale and utilization of older deteriorated bulkers which could cause a repeat of the high loss rate experienced during the 1980's-1990's spate of sinkings.

Relatively new oceangoing foreign-flag bulkers are now carrying various types of cargoes, with about 40% of all vessels in terms of tonnage, and 39.4% in terms of actual ships. These bulkers range in size from single-hold mini-bulkers for river transit to mammoth (*Capesize*) vessels of

Algowood loading
Image from Author's collection

over 200,000-tons deadweight (dwt) which are subject to greater challenges in structural design, and have a capacity too large to transit the Suez and Panama canals with about 93% of them specializing in iron-ore and coal cargoes. A subset of these vessels is reserved for bulkers in the 300,000 tons dwt range that almost always carry iron-ore cargoes around the Capes.

It is known that all are exposed to attritional bulk-cargoes that are very dense, corrosive or abrasive, and present problems such as cargo shifting, *spontaneous combustion*, and cargo saturation that can doom vessels...including Lakers, which do *not* have gas-freeing ventilation of the cargo holds.

From both a global and Great Lakes perspective, terminal ports and major canal waterway systems have some generically-common grounds for limiting bulker design configurations, in that trading vessels are primarily required to have *dimensional* compatibility with their routes and cargo-handling facilities.

And, as may be expected, most ship operators are continually questing for quicker turnaround time which is many times controversial and dangerous, during time-consuming pier-side loading and unloading operations that can have damaging effect on cargo hold and other major hull structure. (i.e. A Laker or oceangoing bulker vessel should be recognized as a subset of overall system capabilities associated with waterway transit limitations, loading, unloading, ballasting, and deballasting. Historically, bulker vessel design is strongly driven by the maritime system requirements in which it operates, rather than vice versa.)

Occasionally ship-management errors can occur that cause a ship to capsize or break in half at a loading pier...even at Great lakes facilities such as Bruce Mines, Ontario, Canada where Algoma Central (Marine) Corporation's Laker-sized (self-unloader) M.V. Algowood ruptured her hull on June 1st 2000 due to poor cargo weight distribution.

Such brief digression is not intended to be extraneous to the subject matter at hand, in consideration of the Author's intent to create a more "open-window" opportunity for readers to frame the Great Lakes bulker and mariner experience within a larger global design and operational universe, having evolutionary overseas marine technology requirements

Algowood rupture, result of improper loading
Image from Author's collection

driven by industrial needs for larger, safe and economically-efficient bulk-cargo hauling innovations contributing to the least operating cost per ton-mile.

In sum, the demand for raw materials by rapidly-expanding industrialization in Far Eastern countries is expected to continue and, by using past initiatives and maritime experiences as prologue for their future, it is possible that the four major shipbuilders and/or governments of Japan, South Korea, The Peoples Republic of China, and Taiwan may have jointly collaborated to further accelerate their merchant marine state of the art...in conjunction with selected Ship Classification Societies and the International Association of Classification Societies (IACS).

This would be a commendable scientific and business model in which commerical American maritime interests should participate, albeit our emaciated merchant vessel design and construction industrial element is in dire straits, and responsible American government maritime agencies receive meager funding support from each succeeding Administration.

To return to the Great lakes "Fitzgerald" scenario, after the Author's short digression on global bulk-cargo vessel-statistics, the USCG Marine Board panelists for the Fitzgerald case are considered to have delinquently impeded liability resolu-

tion by limiting their public hearing scope of enquiry.

An appropriately expanded scope of enquiry could have identified probable cause and provided <u>unequivocal justification for an award of meaningful monetary compensation to aggrieved survivor-family members directly harmed by this tragic event.</u>

In addition, public skepticism appears warranted when observing the Board composition of panelists having <u>zero familiarity or experience</u> with Great Lakes vessels, their in-trade operation, design or construction, or the criticality and conduct of mariner high risk transportation operations when called upon to prosecute urgent, uninterrupted bulk-cargo shipments if contracted to deliver about seventy-thousand tons of ore to keep a major steel mill running about five days.

In this instance, and immediately preceding Fitzgerald's final voyage, it was reported that Captain McSorley's vessel (Fitzgerald-729 feet length) and Captain Cooper's (Anderson-767 feet length) were both <u>directly ordered</u> to proceed to the ore-loading docks at Superior, Wisconsin and to Two Harbors, Minnesota to load cargoes for Zug Island, Michigan and Gary, Indiana respectively.

<u>Even though the structurally-unacceptable material condition of Fitzgerald was known by responsible parties</u> (including shipyard tradesman and Captain McSorley himself).

Their final voyages also began with full anticipation that developing weather conditions would <u>not</u> be favorable.

<u>As footnotes:</u> At that time, there was more shipowner concern about the United States Steel Corporation's older (1952-built) and lengthened (767-foot) S.S. Arthur M. Anderson's structural capability and safety, when operating under "Gitche Gumee's" (Lake Superior) November storm conditions.

However, in retrospect, it does appear that the structurally-improved 120- foot long hull lengthening section (recently installed during Winter 1974-1975 layup), and the spatial navigational separation of the Anderson Laker relative to Fitzgerald's ahead position, may have played protective roles in Anderson's survival under the extreme storm conditions...even though the vessel experienced a severe three-sister boarding-sea wave system that also engulfed the hatch-cover bridge crane and drove her high-mounted lifeboats downward into their saddle supports.

In fact, the Anderson vessel may have later derived even more additional hull strength subsequent to her (1982) conversion from a straight-decker to a stiffer <u>self-loader</u> internal configuration.

In their truncated post-sinking deliberative haste, the USCG and NTSB panelists were neither able to derive curative or preventative technical resolutions, nor formulate objective rationale for the apportionment of fault, culpability or liability.

And, the necessary demarcation between their "inquisitorial" and "accusatorial" inquiry became noticeably blurred during the subject public hearings, that appeared to more appropriately belong under the aegis of the U. S. Department of Justice, and <u>not</u> the-then U.S. Department of The Treasury oversight of assigned United States Coast Guard representatives.

Since the USCG panelists and the NTSB displayed an inability to determine fault, this proved to be a serious deterrent to sound investigatory endeavor, and appears to <u>merit reopening of the Fitzgerald case for courtroom jurisprudence.</u>

Further, belated technical and regulatory body recognition, by the United States Coast Guard (USCG) augmented by American Bureau of Shipping (ABS) technical authorities, should have cautioned that a conventional extrapolation of historical hull structural design empiricism for an advanced-1950's design Laker (such as the S.S. Fitzgerald), would <u>not</u> be compatible with necessary dynamic hull strength requirements, as discussed in the Author's book "For Whom The Bells Toll."

However, the Author is in agreement that his conventional (1958) static analysis estimation of single-plane longitudinal bending stress <u>did</u> yield a safe Spar deck value having dependency on ultimate tensile strength (UTS) of the steel hull materials and welding quality. A finding corroborated by the NTSB.

At a later time, and with advantages from physical observations and production technologies advances in computer-assisted methodologies, it becomes evident that it should <u>now</u> be feasible to comprehensively assess Laker structural instability and fracturing conditions allied to interactive hull bending, springing and twisting characteristics of semi-monocoque (framed) hull structures supported on elastic foundations.

Such requirements should have been more fully researched to assess the increased deleterious effects of "long-ship" flexure caused by magnified multi-axial structural weakness anticipated beyond that yielded by classical (1950's) technical estimations for hogging (upward) and sagging (downward) of her hull...with significant and noticeably amplified vertical, lateral and rotational deflection conditions caused by dynamic load transference while in turbulent seaways.

In effect, during the 1950's era, most responsible technical parties and limited researchers "Did Not Know What They Didn't Know"...<u>and neither did anyone else at that point in time.</u>

To be professionally fair to researchers and designers of that era, this relatively immature (1950's) maritime scientific and technological state of the art was not sufficiently developed in the complex fields of multi-axial hydroelastic hull excitation and response, as necessary for systemic quantification of <u>Laker</u> hull structural bending, springing and twisting structural flexibility. In contrast, naval vessel and aircraft designers, with supporting universities and laboratories were light years ahead of commercial ship developers.

In retrospect, hull flexibility effects were reported initially during the (1977) USCG Marine Board public hearings when then-Third Mate Richard Orgel provided eye-witness testimony of hull springing and bending "Like a Diving Board."

His testimony was made under oath but regrettably the USCG panelists did not appear to be attuned to the subject, nor accepting of such technical input from an eyewitness (*<u>non-degreed</u>*) crew member although he was a licensed Master Mariner with first-hand experience in performing on-board duties...including that of a past-Fitzgerald helmsman having

Captain Richard Orgel

considerable respect for the specialized knowledge held by quote "The slide-rule" engineers.

About that point in time it was only generally known that main sources of hull excitation energy would be produced by vibratory impulses usually traceable to propulsion machinery imbalance and propeller cavitation. Cross-coupling with cyclic hull slamming and the development of hull resonance due to wave forces acting at the bow and having speed, heading and motion dependencies were also factors for consideration.

Under these conditions, the onset of hull vibration and magnification of bending, springing and twisting would be observable and measurable...and would normally be accompanied by hairline cracking, or welded joint separation at stress concentration points, as a harbinger of structural fatigue and shortened operational life.

- 5.0 -
THE "WIGGLY THING"

The late Captain Ernest McSorley's "Wiggly Thing" characterization, of Fitzgerald's disturbing hull flexibility, and then-3rd Mate Richard Orgel's in-service observations eventually had valid technical significance in that:

> The *first* mode of vibration would emerge as torsional, whenever long, slender vessels would twist about their longitudinal axis. The *second* mode of vibration became known as "springing" for susceptible bulk-cargo vessels having a long and limber (flexible) hull, such as Lakers and large ocean-going vessels, that visibly fluctuated upward and downward at about a quarter length (0.25L) from the bow and stern.

When a vessel "springs" the bow and stern deflect upwards, and the mid-length moves downward with cyclic repetition and opposite motion. To restate the mariner terminology of Captain Ernest McSorley, who was aware of the defective structural welding extent and loose hull structure, he had vocally expressed concern regarding the Fitzgerald's gyrating behavior. It is reported that he had colorfully referred to the Fitzgerald hull's structural distortions as "The Wiggly Thing" when refraining from the use of more mariner-like language like "the ship was a piece of sh... (expletive deleted)" during general conversations in the crew's mess room.

Further, it is known that crew engineers did *not* receive rebuke from Captain McSorley when the Fitzgerald's condition was disparaged by their statements such as "The ship was just falling apart," and "The ship was a piece of junk."

These subjective observations and such non-technical statements should serve as a mental barometer of concern and possibly entrapment, when employment on other Lakers may not have been an option due to business cutbacks.

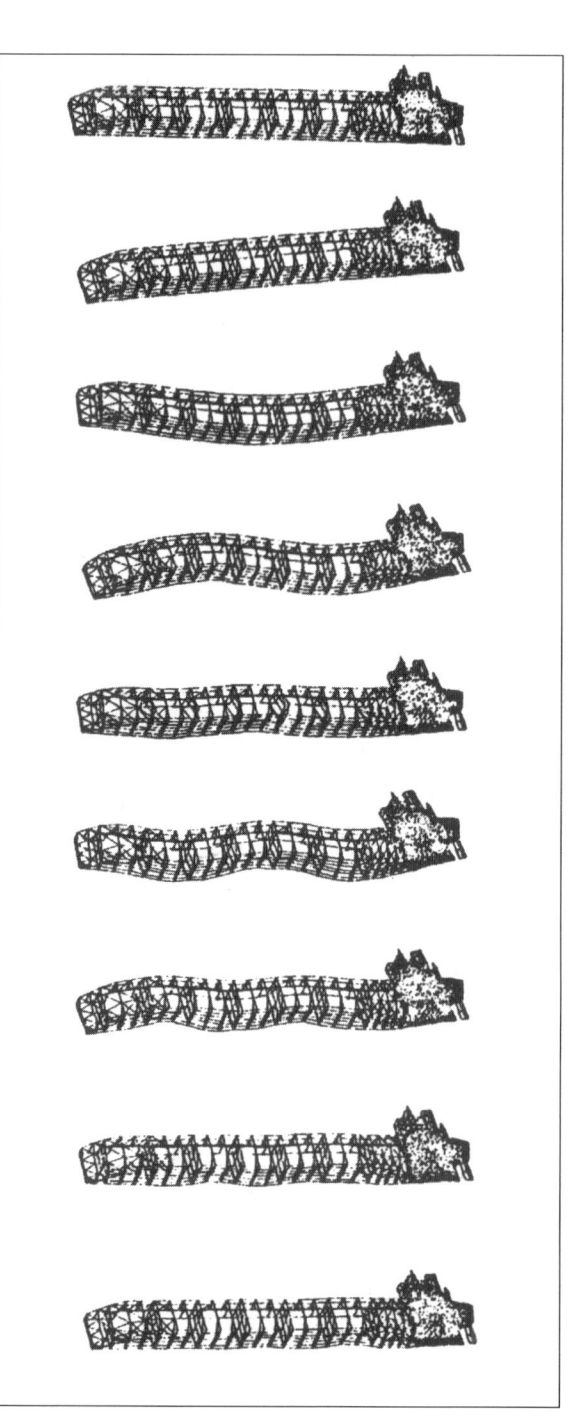

The Wiggly Thing

In corroboration of Captain Orgel's testimony, the Author (ex-GLEW and U.S. Navy naval architect), wishes it to be known that he statically measured Fitzgerald's static hull flexure (1958) under a <u>still-water</u>, <u>lightship</u> condition...and with subsequent eye-witness dynamic observations when walking through the under-deck port and starboard tunnels, during the (September 1958) Lake Erie ship performance trials. The vertical <u>static</u> deflection of the empty ship approximated 1 1/2" per 100 feet of ship length.

At a more recent time (1969) another mature and experienced graduate naval architect actually rode in Fitzgerald's cellular double bottom (CDB) ballast tank to witness and measure "oil-canning" flexure of the Centerline Vertical Keel (CVK) while underway, together with broken welds to which additional structural stiffening was temporarily added. The CVK is considered to be a major longitudinal member serving as the Fitzgerald's "spinal column," with the transverse CDB structural floors considered as connective "ribs" (to the CVK) for frame and boundary shell attachments. Their omitted and deferred repair welding was noted in CDB and other water ballast tank spaces having limited worker and inspector access.

The Author is pleased that at least two degreed naval architects eventually validated Captain Ogel's (non-degreed) public hearing testimony.

There is now credible documentary evidence that the late Captain Ernest McSorley and other "non-degreed" crew members had also expressed deep concern over the vessel's extremely limber condition during his (1972-1975) command. Notably when USCG and ABS inspectors discovered and reported structural weaknesses attributable to extensive "loose-keel" non-welded and partly-welded steel hull structure throughout the cellular (7-feet high) double bottom tankage having contiguous side ballast tank compartments...during their regulatory hull inspections (winter 1972-1973) in a shipyard.

Not all required welding repairs were shipowner-authorized for accomplishment and, in keeping with the decaying structural trend, there was corrosion increase and more near-term weld joint failures. Severe hull flexing was not abated.

It is known that, shortly before the Fitzgerald loss, it was estimated that defective (loose) weld joints extended linearly over <u>4,000 feet</u> of critical ballast tank structure, and that the shipowners deferred execution of these welding repairs even though the necessary work was reportedly "Red-Flagged" by USCG inspectors...with a strong recommendation that shipyard departure be <u>denied</u> until corrective hull structural restoration actions were accomplished.

However, higher USCG authority, in collaboration with private sector executives, discussed the critical urgency for the Fitzgerald and Anderson to depart without further delay, and Captain McSorley (who

Image Courtesy of G.L.S.H.S.

had vocalized concerns about his vessel's material condition) and Captain Cooper proceeded as directed.

The S.S. Edmund Fitzgerald experienced hull breakup and sinking *only 10 days later* when <u>overloaded</u> with iron-ore cargo at the authorized deeper Winter draft; <u>without</u> the necessary repair of defective structural welding, and while in transit under severe storm conditions on Lake Superior.

ANALYSIS AND SYNTHESIS

While written and oral data collection were definitely prerequisites for CRA's evidence formation, their selection for Fitzgerald's casualty analysis and synthesis required carefully prioritized consideration of failure modes and effects attributable to human error or ship or shore side support system malfunctions, steelwork and equipment manufacturing quality, and unforeseen environmental cause majeure events.

With such a rationalized approach, a veritable kaleidoscope of data elements was pragmatically reduced in number without sacrificing certitude.

And, lest it be forgotten, most human beings (with and without academic degrees) do make contributions that are vital to every phase of ship design, construction and operation...as advanced in the Japanese production management model by the late Dr. W. Edwards Deming and Dr. David Durand (USA) in their promotion of statistical quality control having worker participation in on-site Quality Circles.

For business success, the maxim applies that: <u>"Man is a most versatile creation that can be mass-produced by unskilled labor."</u> It is deep-rooted throughout totally-committed industries and should have enduring validity. And, although shipbuilding and repair are universally recognized as labor-intensive occupations, a precedent philosophy of dedicating one's physical body to the workplace and leaving cerebral capabilities outside shipyard gates is an anachronism to be discontinued.

Images Courtesy of U.S.C.G.

CREWS BATTLE SEAS TO ASSESS ALASKA OIL SPILL

Reminder

Malaysian Oceangoing 73,000-Ton Dry Cargo Freighter
"Selendang Ayu" Hull Separates On Grounding In Bering Sea
with Soy Bean And Oil Cargoes.

Launched on September 8th 1997.
Built in China for Global Marine Ventures.

Grounded and Split on December 8th 2004.
<u>With loss of mariner and crashed helicopter crew lives.</u>

The hull fracturing of this relatively young vessel serves as a reminder that ship structural criteria, design challenges and operation should continue to be addressed by merchant marine technical communities.

- 6.0 -
THE CRUX OF THE CASE

Casualty Research Associates (CRA) have documented discoveries that provide the necessary factual evidence necessary to establish credibility and culpability in proving that the shipowner, charterer and U.S. Government regulatory bodies knowingly and unknowingly facilitated and condoned abuse of the S.S. Edmund Fitzgerald... and with endangerment of crew and safety by overloading, and neglecting to perform necessary repairs and maintenance for safe operations.

With such prima facie evidence now available to unquestionably identify the shipowner's negligence, in overloading an unrepaired vessel not retrofitted with additional hull reinforcement commensurate with an authorized increase in draft, and not maintaining and repairing the Fitzgerald in a safe operating condition, then that party appears liable for most of the loss suffered...including meaningful court-awarded compensation for surviving families of the crew members and the rescinding of any restrictive (gag-order) financial affidavits executed between the shipowner and bereaved survivor families.

Since U.S. Coast Guard inspectors are charged with ensuring that vessels are routinely inspected to specific standards on a scheduled basis before issuance of a Certificate of Inspection, and may board vessels at any time, they are expected to exercise strong oversight authority in their enforcement of inspection rules and regulations, but should not be held directly accountable for the appropriateness of inspection criteria standards to which they are expected to work.

These expectations were not fully realized during Fitzgerald's lifetime and the current "United States Coast Guard's Management of the Marine Casualty Investigation Program" did not receive a favorable report by the Office of the Inspector General (OIG) in their report to Congress dated May 19th 2008 (Appendix 111).

During the Congressional Hearings, testimony affirmed that:
The National Transportation Safety Board ("NTSB") has <u>primacy</u> over the Coast Guard in the conduct of marine casualty investigations having shared responsibilities. The "NTSB" is required to bring together all interested parties, including the Coast Guard to examine all available evidence, and is required to act at any time in the aftermath of marine casualty should any disagreement require authoritative resolution. (While the NTSB and Coast Guard may have similar responsibilities, different processes and different objectives may be present).

During the Congressional Hearings, testimony provided objective critique of:
- Deficiencies in on-line reporting of casualty reports.
- Shortages of qualified, trained, and experienced Coast Guard Marine Casualty investigators ("IO's").
- Status of personnel currently assigned to "IO" billets and those with "IO" certifications not assigned to "IO" billets.
- Hindrance of marine casualty investigations by unqualified personel; conduct at inappropriate levels; ineffective management of a substantial backlog of investigations needing review and closure.

In November 2006, the Coast Guard HQ had a backlog of over 4,000 investigations of which almost 2,500 (58%) had been opened and awaiting review for more than six (6) months. Only one person was assigned to expedite the process.

The foregoing outlines long-standing deficiencies that have (and are) <u>limiting regulatory effectiveness</u> for the <u>safety of commercial vessels and their mariners</u>...as responsible activities operate under ever-increasing mission responsibilities, budgetary and staffing limitations imposed by Congress.

In view of this, the S.S. Edmund Fitzgerald catastrophic sinking (and others cited herein) definitely call the Board's investigatory hearing standards and procedures into question.

A (Fitzgerald) rehearing is considered to be merited to include, but not be limited to, over-dependency on heuristic (Rule of Thumb) extrapolation of historic empirical data...without adequate supportive Research, Development, Test and Evaluation (RDT&E) for hull structural design, inclusive of:

> - Initial (1950') hull structural design (for Fitzgerald) which was overly-dependent upon heuristic extrapolations considerably beyond prevailing practices for smaller and less powerful Lakers, many of which failed to survive in Great Lakes service. Flawed and technical assumptions germane to this over-extended design practice resulted in a shortened-life, and a weakened hull having severe multi-axial bending and springing as a precursor to near-term onset of structural fatigue and catastrophic failure.
> - Cargo overloading authorization and distribution monitoring.
> - Absence of additional hull and cargo hatch cover/hatch coaming reinforcements to provide compensatory immersion strength commensurate with deeper draft loading authorizations.
> - Unsafe and incomplete structural disrepair and maintenance conditions.

As stated from a technically-credible engineering perspective, significant hull flexure was statically measured under still-water and lightship (unladen) conditions by this (degreed naval architect) author at GLEW shipyard dockside, shortly following the Fitzgerald's (1958) launching. Also, dynamic underway observations of hull flexing were made by the observer, when walking through the under-deck port and starboard tunnels, during (September 1958) Lake Erie ship performance trials.

A number of other technically credentialed and experienced maritime industry subcontractors also performed surveys over the years, and some witnessed Fitzgerald's hull bending and springing. They also saw her critical hull weld joint deficiencies and made reinforcement recommendations... which were not always followed because of ship scheduling commitments or extensive maintenance and repair expense implications.

Further discoveries (1969) of continuing welding deficiencies, structural failures and unsatisfactory weld joint fit-up gaps between abutting bottom-shell and other steel plating were made by a qualified naval architectural company under contract to the Oglebay Norton charterer. *The cited naval architect contractor was terminated and replaced by one who gave second-order priority to hull safety and technical correctness.*

Unconnected welds, including the critical Center Vertical Keel (CVK) and longitudinal side keelsons to the inside surface of the bottom shell plating and other structures were gouged out and re-welded, only to have the same structural failures reoccur in subsequent years, up to and including the time of Fitzgerald's sinking.

Under these conditions, the vessel was literally heard to emit audible groaning while underway, moreso than other Lakers, due to overloaded weaknesses and defective structural connections. Therefore, with Fitzgerald loaded to maximum Winter draft and without compensatory hull structural reinforcement, she displayed many characteristics of a 35,000 ton neglected-behemoth.

From a clinician point of view, the Fitzgerald did not have human physiology attributes but it was apparent that she did have distinctive "vital signs" to communicate advance warning of physical straining.

On some occasions, it was physically possible to insert a shovel or crowbar into excessively-gapped weld joints for the removal of unconsumed welding rods and miscellaneous detritus, that were improperly disposed of prior to vessel to delivery from the GLEW shipyard and subsequent to recurring life-cycle repair work that required powerful jacking assistance for forced weld-gap closure...which could have incurred "locked-in" prestressing.

Within the shipbuilding industry, this waste disposal practice is generally known as weld "slugging" to enable an accelerated output of minimally-inspected high-production welds, that are usually accomplished by welders receiving higher piece-work earnings. This practice is considered to provide a first-hand illustration of the truism that:

"Competitive industrial greed, without adequate training and control morals, can frequently bring out the best performance in business entity accounting "bottom-lines" but may also encourage the worst traits of human beings."

Such a truism appears to have had merit, when one considers that GLEW shipyard welders were reputed to have had a higher performance output of about 125 feet of weld deposition per day, compared to other Great Lakes shipyards reportedly producing only 65 feet per day.

Apart from productivity and fabrication methodology differences, additional consideration should also have been given to the mix of short-term experienced and lesser-trained welders who were not hired until the ship construction contract was awarded...when it was reported that the production workforce was rapidly expanded by over 1,000+ workers, with "hire and fire" expectations.

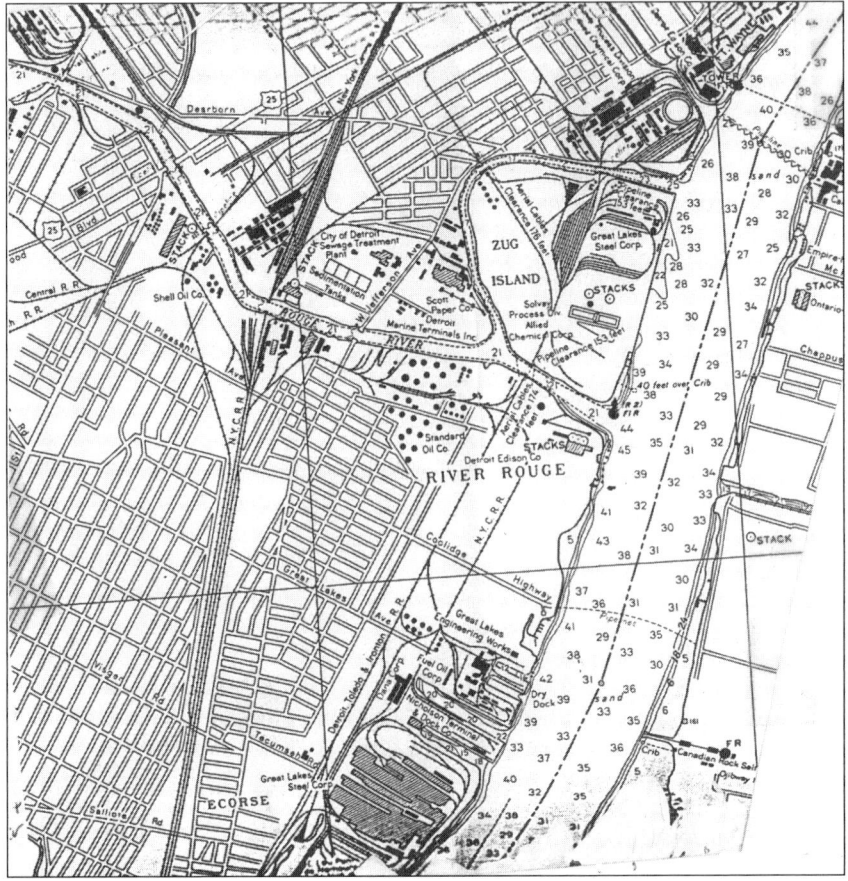

*River Rouge, Michigan G.L.E.W. Shipyard site, U.S. Army Corps of Engineers,
U.S. Lake Survey - Detroit River, Chart No. 41 (1958)*

Images from Author's collection

A Metamorphosis - The Great Lakes Yacht Club.
(formerly the Great Lakes Engineering Works Shipyard)
River Rouge, Michigan
Image courtesy of River Rouge Historical Museum

Top: Keel laying August 7th, 1957
Bottom: Side Balast Tank <u>Module</u> one side (rotated 90°), K +4 weeks.
Images from Dossin Museum Collection

Top: K +12 weeks
Bottom: K + 16 weeks
Images from Dossin Museum Collection

- 7.0 -
A REMINISCENT SOLILOQUY

With dedication to S.S. Edmund Fitzgerald, her mariners and the shipyard workforce. As with any soliloquy an orator reveals inner thoughts to a specific audience but few others, and may appear to be speaking to himself.

In acceptance that the sands of time will eventually obscure our human memories, in a similar manner to the bottom sediment of Lake Superior blurring recollections of the Edmund Fitzgerald hull remains and her entombed mariners, the writer considers it wise to seize the present God-given moments to recall observations made during and after technical employment with the Great Lakes Engineering Works (GLEW) shipyard.

Upon arrival in March 1958 I must candidly admit that my first impression of the shipyard facility (which started operations in 1903, as did Wright brothers with flight in Kittyhawk, North Carolina) was quite uninspiring.

Mr. Edmund Fitzgerald and the S.S. Edmund Fitzgerald

- 7.1 -
PREFABRICATION & WELDING

There was only one (1) ship assembly berth, with a North-South orientation which required shipyard tradesmen (welders et al) to dimensionally compensate for steelwork expansion and contraction when exposed to sunlight temperature variations from East-West sun repositioning during daylight hours.

This assembly berth was located in parallel with a prefabrication platform to support off-hull modular construction and the maximizing of "down-hand" continuous welding for spar deck and other steel plating sub-assemblies in a flat position.

Automatic Submerged Arc Welding (SUBARC) was widely used in the joining of steel plating by heating with an arc between a bare metal electrode or electrodes and the work at hand. External pressure was not used and filler metal was supplied from an electrode or from a supplementary welding rod. The arc was shielded by a blanket of granular material on the work.

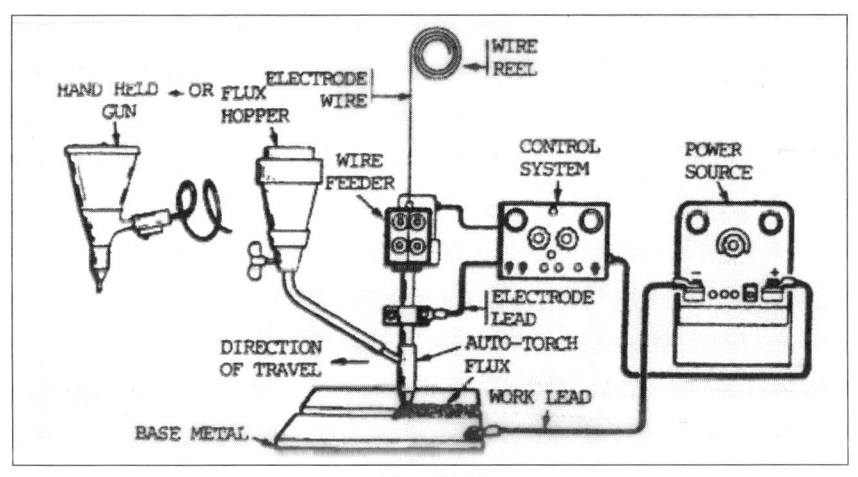

Flux Weld
Image from Author's Collection

Additionally, other weld tacking and continuous welding processes were performed, including ergonomically-challenging overhead welding which was accomplished on spar deck panel undersides after shipboard positioning over hull structural supporting frameworks, and subsequent to pneumatic steel chipping-hammer operators ensuring satisfactory weld joint surface preparation.

*Top: Prefabricated Cellular Double Bottom (CDB) Water Ballast Tank Structure
Bottom: Prefabricated Cellular Double Bottom (CDB)
positioned on Bottom Shell Plating*
Image from Author's Collection

- 7.2 -
SHIPYARD ENVIRONMENT

In hindsight, difficult working conditions are known to have raised questions regarding the questionable *pre-delivery* quality of some welded joints and their fit-up, that would have contributed to severe hull "bending and springing" flexibilities.

And, in addition to considering humanities in the workplace, the weld production circumstances should have been given more technical questioning as an "Achilles Heel" relative to life-cycle cracking, hull fatigue, and compromised structural integrity, including:

- Steel fabrication processes, requiring progressive material inspection, cutting, handling and alignment which were characteristically labor-intensive requiring frequent oversight and welded fit-up adjustments. Efficient planning and scheduling were key to the following labor-intensive work elements.

- Selective temporary tack-welding preceding continuous manual welding closure of abutting weld joint root gap openings of 1/8th inch unless otherwise specified. This practice was found to be necessary for controlling large fabricated steel panel alignments subject to dimensional shrinkage and/or distortion, to compensate for ambient environmental temperature variations coupled with welding heat-affected zone concentrations.

- Control of the fit-up shrinkage of panel sub-assemblies by judicious relocations of on-board welders to execute staged sequencing of welding operations, prior to the lateral transfer of unitized panels to, and mating up with, supportive hull framing structures erected on the ship assembly berth.

- A variety of fillet, single-vee and double-vee continuous joints were made under reasonably accessible automated and manual welding conditions. Although some thicker-plate, requiring deep full-penetration welding did evoke quality concerns. On the other hand, constraining welding circumstances within severely space-restricted compartments proved to be ergonomically and physiologically (inhumanely) demanding. Poor ventilation and primitive lighting were endemic to the environment of welders working in cellular double-bottom (CDB) ballast tanks and other confining compartments that were hazardous to safety and human endurance.

- All welding was <u>in need of proper stress relief</u> to prevent critical fracture according to Mr. August G. Hebel Jr., president American Society for Testing metals. In a letter to the Detroit Free Press in October 1976, he cited USCG photographs and cracked weld evidence for Fitzgerald that were <u>never repaired</u> and the use of riveted plates to "patch up" faulty welds.

Without question, the GLEW shipyard allowed the Author to gain professional insight by facilitating initial exposure to the basic and innovative capabilities of a historically-experienced Great Lakes shipbuilder, and an opportunity to participate in Lake Erie trials.

Today, it is highly probable that the Author is the sole remaining naval architect of the (1958) GLEW hull design staff who is still available and willing to support investigative efforts made with altruistic intent.

Like the GLEW shipyard, both Furness (England) and Davie (Canada) shipbuilders where the Author trained and worked were of longstanding. They were technologically progressive, and had multiple building positions for a variety of large and small merchant ships benefiting from then-advanced production processes that enabled successful competition in the <u>domestic and international maritime marketplaces, and without government subsidy.</u>

However, with deference to the various shipyard limitations, the GLEW shipyard Planning and Production Department performed an apparently commendable feat by achieving a "Fitzgerald" keel-laying to launch time of only forty-four (44) weeks...with follow-on construction for almost-sister straight-decker Lakers (S.S. "Herbert C. Jackson" and the S.S. "Arthur B. Homer") closely behind.

The GLEW shipyard industrial environment was a different experience for the Author but, on the positive side, it did facilitate a memorable introduction to Laker operations and the practices and capabilities of tradition-bound Great Lakes shipbuilders who were exposed to raw, open-air seasonal weather conditions and subjected to space limitations, and under-capitalization.

As stated in the book "For Whom The Bells Toll" on Page 41, "It certainly appeared that the preliminary design "train" had left the station" in advance of my coming aboard," but this did not preempt objective design review. The Author's concerns were reinforced as he explored questionable Fitzgerald compliance with safety precepts that are integral with USCG Load Line Regulations and which included, but were not limited to:

Precept (a)
"That the hull is strong enough for all anticipated seaways."

The Author determined (in 1958) that quantification of Great Lakes wave spectra and force structure had received minimal research and government funding beyond a awareness that these wave systems usually had shorter crest-to-crest wave spacings, with heights relatively greater than those for open-ocean waves. Therefore, structsural design loading design assumptions were dubious. He also determined (in 1958) that, although the pioneering Fitzgerald was classified as a "Steamer Having Superior Design And Operation Features Engaged On Great Lakes Voyages," her structural design was predicated on past experience and traditional heuristic (rules of thumb) reasoning and extrapolations above and beyond the characteristics of smaller, lesser-powered and slower Lakers of earlier generations.

Better Shipbuilding Times
at Furness Shipyard
(140 Ships)
1918-1968

Shipbuilding Berth modified For M.V. Derbyshire Construction and End-Launching

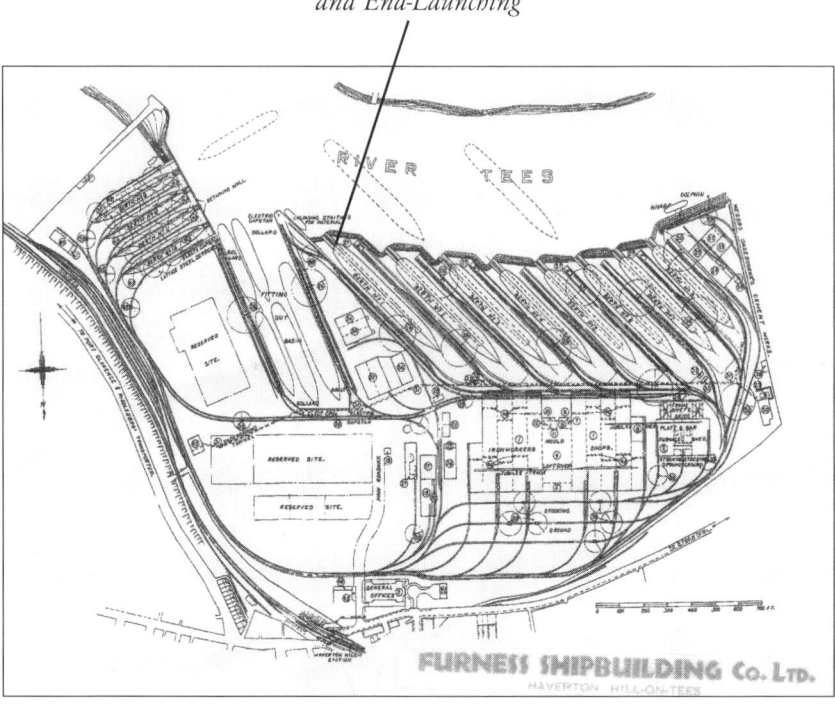

Without the benefit of collateral Research, Development and Test (RDT&E), the Fitzgerald's hull structure is considered to have failed by *ductile* fracture while excessively flexing on the lake surface, and under severe storm conditions while overloaded. Iin-service, the Fitzgerald experienced significant, visible and debilitating hull envelope "bending and springing" deflection, welding and material failures, and a need for demanding USCG and shipowner surveillance.

Precept (b)
"That the ship is designed and operated with proper stability."

In contrast with this general USCG vessel safety precept, the GLEW hull design management <u>denied</u> the Author's (1958) authorization requests to proceed with the development of:

- A manual for loading and unloading of various cargoes and operational ballasted conditions
- A procedural plan to conduct a conventional naval architectural "Inclining Experiment" to determine the vessel's metacentric height (GM), which would affirm the center of gravity position and support proper stability calculations for cargoes of various densities and loading conditions.

In both instances, the rationales for denial had similarities as follows:
(1) "There were *no* promulgated USCG Load Line Regulation requirements, and therefore GLEW would not receive shipowner reimbursement should they proceed.
(2) Lakers have adequate stability due to their "boxy" hull form.
(3) Vessel masters would *not* use an office prepared manual.

Precept (c)
"That the hull is watertight to the freeboard deck."

Traditional non-water-tight cargo-hold *screen* bulkheads negated GLEW compliance for internal water tightness compartmentation.

Aerial view of Davie shipyard in 1958
Image from Author's Collection

Precept (d)
"That the hull has sufficient reserve buoyancy for seaworthiness."

Fitzgerald's reserve buoyancy was diminished subsequent to the USCG 1973 Load Line Amendment authorizing decreases in freeboard (deeper draft) to enhance cargo-carrying capacity and operator revenues.

It was estimated that the original design had sufficient reserve buoyancy remaining for damaged condition survival, after breaching of three (3) ballast tanks on one side.

Precept (e)
"That the topside area is properly fitted so as to be capable of being made weather-tight for all anticipated seaways."

Precept (f)
"That protection for the movement of crew on the weather decks at sea is provided".

No positive or negative comment, other than an observation where shipowner, designer and mariner sensibilities should have professionally overcome the absence of USCG Load Line Regulation safety requirements by:

> - Preparation of vessel cargo load distribution manual, in loaded, loading and ballasted conditions and with consideration of available Loadicator instrumentation having pilothouse readout.
> - Conduct of an Inclining Experiment to determine the vessel's metacentric height, (GM) and vertical center of gravity (VCG) position.
> - Preparation of trim and stability calculations.
> - Installation of a fathometer to track lake floor topography shoaling clearance; for verification of bottom clearances alongside loading docks; and when navigating restrictive waterways.
> - Outfitting addition of an Emergency Position Indicating Beacon (EPIRB) to shorten shipwreck detection time lapse.
> - Development and installation of mariner emergency escape modules, or other <u>21st-century</u> devices, to replace vintage technology lifeboats, which are known to require hazardous accident-prone handling during launching and mariner recovery when deployed in heavy sea conditions.

Considerable testimony was received concerning the use of primary lifesaving equipment. Without exception, <u>the witnesses expressed considerable doubt</u> that lifeboats could have been successfully launched by the crew of the vessel under the weather conditions which existed at the time Fitzgerald was lost. A Great Lakes Registered Pilot testified: "...I have said that if the damn ship is going to go down, I would get in my bunk and pull the blankets over my head and say, 'Let her go,' because there was no way of launching the boats."

The Author also recalled other professional observations and experiences during tenure in the minimally-equipped GLEW hull design office where he was able to monitor Fitzgerald's construction progress and support vessel side-launching prepara-

tions, and to develop registered gross and net tonnage calculations.

On an ad-hoc basis with technical curiosity motivation, estimates of longitudinal hull bending stress and deflection, were made, <u>using on-site hull measurements</u> and conventional (1950's) methodologies.

The Author was privileged to participate in the "Fitzgerald's" Lake Erie performance trials September 13th 1958, when he was able to observe dynamic hull flexure.

A more detailed account is presented in the author's companion book *"For Whom The Bells Toll"* which was published in the year 2006 by the Dorrance Publishing Company, Pittsburgh.

At that (1958) point in time, the "Big Fitz" business initiative was receiving a considerable number of maritime accolades. She was owned by Northwestern Mutual Life Insurance Company, Wisconsin as an investment, and then conveyed to Oglebay Norton Company, Columbia Transportation Company Division, and it's insurers as a Bareboat Charter with the latter responsibility for manning, victualing, supplies and in all respects maintaining the vessel to a high standard.

There is no recall that anyone ever envisioned her as a future national icon, or if anyone openly suspected shortfalls in her advanced structural design approach, fabrication quality and life-cycle maintenance…all of which had some deficiencies that individually or collectively are considered contributory to terminating her high-performing seventeen (17-year bulk-cargo carrying lifetime).

During her heyday, and regrettably after her loss, commercial interests fostered a "mystique and mystery" charisma for the "Fitz"… subsequent to <u>inconclusive</u> outcomes from official investigations and the trail-blazing private ventures of others.

The author et al., personally found such diversions most distressing from the point of view of bereaved survivor families who are (still) believed to be entitled to psychological closure and more equitable financial compensation for their losses, since newly-discovered "probable-cause" grounds appear to display credible evidence to justify <u>a rehearing,</u> presided over by the U.S. Department of Justice…and <u>not</u> by governmental regulatory bodies having inherent conflicts of interest.

This cogent latter justification would ensure unbiased, <u>Rule of Law</u> adjudication relative to the Fitzgerald ship owner's negligence, and obviate any circumstances wherein the official (USCG) regulators would be unable to pontificate on situations that were caused (in part) by their own technical criteria, ineptness, interpersonal collusion, and lack of diligence.

Also, cadres of budget-constrained technocrats and ship owners having a professional ethic obligation to conduct advanced research for the avoidance of hull structural failures, and to correct (through selective retrofitting) any deficiencies that may be inherent in the design, construction or operation of completed and future vessels.

Many (known and unknown) factors are believed to have contributed to Fitzgerald's *post*-delivery weld joint failure events. It is known that considerable deterioration was neither revealed nor corrected, during the <u>deferral of ship maintenance expense</u> and shipyard stand down time which could have detracted from productive, revenue-earning ore-carrying commitments.

While the late President Woodrow Wilson stated that "The Business of America is business," an (unspoken) corollary to this is that "There is usually a consequential price to be paid" as evidenced by Fitzgerald's catastrophic loss.

The current preponderance of factual evidence was systematically accumulated by Casualty Research Associates (CRA), subsequent to the initial USCG discovery and later "red-flagging" of (unrepaired) critical weld defects, in internal ballast tankage (and other compartments containing mud and other detritus)… whenever "mudded out" for the accomplishment of regulatory visual structural inspections.

Nevertheless, the Author's sentiments for this hitherto unexplained disaster have never diminished and, since there is no claim to *locus standi* that would legitimize any views on fault, civil or criminal liabilities, the preponderance of Fitzgerald evidence is dependent on the veracity and credibility of informational sources at various levels.

The Author's judicial mindset, tempered by a broad private sector career background and governmental service, has also facilitated rational and objective perspectives to be given balanced consideration...with bias toward approaches amenable to the analysis and synthesis of factual informational resources. As opposed to alternative mechanisms, wherein one may envelope one's thoughts in the "coin-of-the-realm" popular mystery and mystique, as practiced and broadcast by those having privately-held collusive, self-serving arrangements for Fitzgerald matters other than technical enquiry and grief for loved ones.

- 8.0 -
COMPARISONS AND CONTRASTS
- 8.1 -
SHIPYARDS AND PRACTICES

Many GLEW employee workplace situations were not user-friendly and were quite different from the merchant ship design and construction environment, where I served a five (5)-year apprenticeship with the reputable Furness Shipbuilding Company in England (1947-1952)...and that of the Davie Shipbuilding Company in Quebec, Canada where I worked in preliminary design (1956-1958) after crossing the Atlantic "pond."

The (GLEW) shipyard hull and machinery technical staffs were located in a small, bi-level, non-air conditioned building...where we all endured a shortage of creature comforts and normal design office equipment. It cannot be forgotten that both areas were unhealthily infiltrated by airborne deposits from nearby steel-making industries, unless buffered by the closing of windows under sweltering heat conditions.

Regardless of the physically and mentally challenging conditions, the shipbuilders' pride and camaraderie is believed to have survived.

In this vein, the following is offered to forthrightly share some thoughts as possibly the last remaining naval architect member of the Great Lakes Engineering Works (GLEW) hull design staff, and as a rare "insider" to introduce technical and humanitarian points of view to the shipyard framework of reference.

- 8.2 -
DESIGN CONSIDERATIONS

The "Fitzgerald" was one of a few remaining American-flagged, American-manned vessels operating under the protective Jones Act, without government subsidies or foreign competition. The Act requires American ownership, shipyard design construction and crewing, for Great Lakes service and to cargo terminals along the St. Lawrence River.

Oceangoing and coastal operations were <u>not</u> authorized since she was classified as:

> A steamer having superior design and operation features engaged on Great Lakes voyages, *and* as a Laker, she was designed to <u>lesser-demanding</u> structural and other technical requirements supposedly compatible with her working environment.

Conventional estimations of Laker structural effectiveness, under high-impact damaging conditions of mechanized loading and unloading (at dockside) with attendant attritional effects on cargo hold bulkheads and CDB floors, were worthy of special consideration... especially in locations having potential for undetectable (i.e.non-inspectable) fabrication defects.

Initially undetectable *pre-delivery deficiencies* were (later) repeatedly given recognition during in-service inspections by USCG and ABS inspectors; welding repair cadres; Fitzgerald crew members: expert consultants et al., who voiced their concerns over unusually-large hull flexures and the need to make repair welds (and re-welds) to cracked and/or separated critical joints in Fitzgerald's hull structure.

The NTSB Marine Accident Report contrasted Fitzgerald's casualty situation with other in-service Lakers and found that: "The Fitzgerald was one of a fleet of 14 to 18 vessels operated by the Columbia Transportation Division between 1972 and 1977. The USCG casualty records for the company fleet did <u>not</u> reveal any heavy weather damage during this period."

Author comment: Contrasted vessels did <u>not</u> have Fitzgerald's hull structural configuration nor were the environmental conditions or locations identical.

In the Author's book, this element of our maritime community is referred to as the *"Silent Service"* which is a term usually reserved for submariners who are vital for national security and do operate in a military harm's way. It is possible to perceive similarities with the silent and almost invisible nature of Laker operations, that contribute to the <u>national defense industrial base,</u> within our *"Eighth Sea"* having the nations *Fourth Coastline*...while coping with a hazardous environmental type of harm's way. And, although Lakers do not carry weaponry, history has shown that our wartime and peacetime industrial economies would be unable to feed the voracious appetite of steel mills and power generation plants without support from the Great lakes maritime fleet.

Bulker Efficiency Contrasts.

It is remarkable that oceangoing bulkers of emergent Far Eastern industrialized maritime fleets are advancing their economics by significantly improving the technological state of the art for mammoth vessels using extended global trading routes.

While oceangoing bulker hulls continue to increase in size, they are expected to retain their full (boxy) hull form, with a high block coefficient to maximize cargo-carrying capacity...which will, in turn, cause sacrifices in transit speeds (i.e. Bulkers will continue to be slow-speed vessels).

By comparing a vessel's cargo-carrying capability in terms of deadweight (dwt) tonnage relative to an unladen weight, is one way of qualitatively estimating bulk cargo carrying efficiency.

For example: A relatively small oceangoing bulker (35,000 to 55,000 tons dwt) is estimated to carry about five (5) times its own weight, whereas the gigantic *Capesize* (200,000+ tons dwt) vessels are capable of carrying about eight (8) times their own weight. Bulkers over 300,000 tons dwt. are a special subset of *Capesize* and mainly carry iron ore cargoes throughout the world.

In contrast the Fitzgerald and larger Lakers fall short, since their hull dimensions are severely constrained by our intra-continent locks and waterway navigational limitations...and are therefore unable to significantly enhance their cargo-enhancing revenues.

From a global competition perspective, the lower-cost per ton-mile coupled with lesser labor and overhead rates of Far Eastern Industrial nations could bring about (further) near-term devastation of our steel-producing and waterborne raw material transportation business communities.

Therefore, from an econometric standpoint of view, it would appear Laker owner/operator executive initiatives may become compelled to explore (unidentified) higher-value cargo transportation options from mineral-rich natural processed and manufactured resources within the Great Lakes industrial system. Possibly, in technology-transfer collaboration with Far Eastern maritime nations and their Ship Classification Societies, future Lakers may benefit from technologies and methodologies already safely supporting bulkers ranging from 35,000 to over 300,000 tons cargo deadweight.

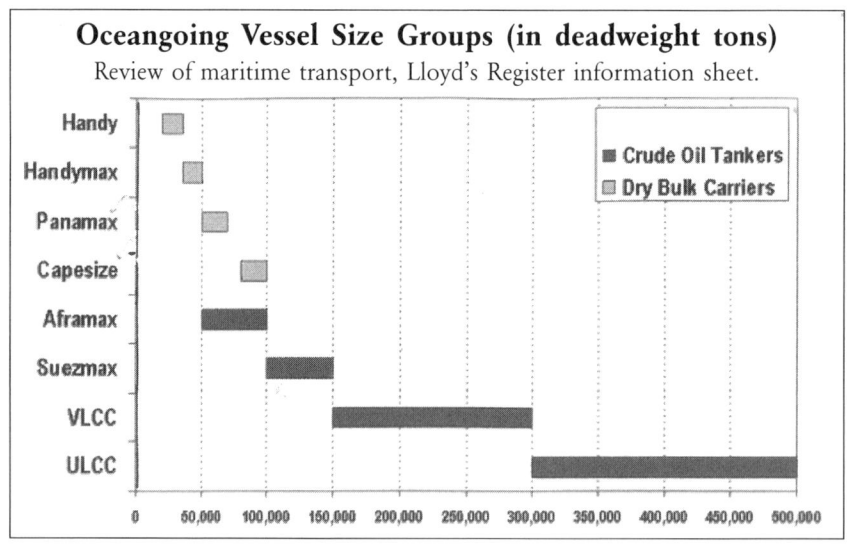

Oceangoing Vessel Size Groups (in deadweight tons)
Review of maritime transport, Lloyd's Register information sheet.

Image Courtesy of United Nations Council on Trading Development (UNCTD)

Major ship size groups include:

Handyman and Handymax: traditionally the workhorses of the dry bulk market, the Handy and more recent Handymax types remain popular ships with less than 50,000 dwt. This category is also used to define small-sized oil tankers.

Panamax: Currently represents the largest acceptable size to transit the Panama Canal, which can be applied to both freighters and tankers; lengths are restricted to a maximum of 965 feet and widths slightly more then 105 feet. The average size of such a ship is about 65,000 dwt. Enlargement planned 2015.

Capesize: Refers to rather ill-defined standard which have the common characteristic Of being incapable of using the Panama Suez canals, not necessarily because of their materials, such as iron or and coal. As a result, "Capesize" vessels transit via Cape Horn (South America) or the Cape of Good Hope (South Africa). Their size ranges between 80,000 and 175,000 dwt.

Aframax: A tanker of standard size between 75,000 and 115,000 dwt. The largest tanker size in the AFRA (Average Freight Rate Assessment) tanker rate system.

Suezmax: This standard, which represents the limitations of the Suez Canal, has Evolved. Before 1967, the Suez Canal could only accommodate tanker ships with a Maximum of 80,000 dwt. The canal was closed between 1967 and 1975 because of the Israel - Arab conflict. Once reopened in 1975, the Suezmax capacity went to 150,000 dwt. An enlargement to enable the canal to accommodate 200,000 dwt tankers is being considered.

VLCC: Very Large Crude Carriers, 150,000 to 320,000 dwt in size. They offer a good Flexibility for using terminals since many can accommodate their draft. They are used in ports that have depth limitations, mainly around the Mediterranean, West Africa and the North Sea. They can be ballasted through the Suez Canal.

ULCC: Ultra Large Crude Carriers, 300,000 to 550,000 dwt in size. Used for carrying Crude oil on long haul routes from the Persian Gulf to Europe, America and East Asia, Via the Cape of Good Hope of the Strait of Malacca. The enormous size of these vessels require custom built terminals.

- 8.3 -
DESIGN PREMISING

By looking into a rear-view mirror of the 1950's era, it is evident that Laker designers and Great Lakes shipyards were for many years comfortably ensconced and insulated by tradition-bound precedents, using semi-empirical and rule-of-thumb heuristic reasoning and labor-intensive ship design and undercapitalized construction practices.

Maritime historians may recall that a transition from riveted to welded Laker hulls began during wartime in the 1940's, and brought with it some of the production advantages and problems experienced by coastal shipyards engaging in the wartime mass-production of a (5,400-ship) merchant fleet.

Hull structure failures did occur and, while Henry J. Kaiser's "Coffin Ships" continued to be delivered, their plating and welding operations became subject to government agency research. Their outcomes were not all conclusive, because of the many metallurgical and workplace variables involved, although many operational ship casualties were found to occur at low temperatures within a temperature high of 67 degrees F to a low of zero degrees F. The majority of hull fractures started at air or water temperatures between 30 and 45 degree F.

In more-recent times (1950's) the GLEW shipyard advanced the hull fabrication state of the art for Lakers, by introducing welded <u>modular construction</u> productivity increases for building the S.S. Edmund Fitzgerald and her two almost-sister vessels. Albeit selected locations retained riveted connections for alignment compensation and "crack-arrester" mitigation benefit, should welded plating butt joints fail and propagate.

In those days, and prior, there was a designer's "comfort zone," when slower-speed and lesser-powered Laker and oceangoing bulk-cargo vessels shared a common hull slenderness Length to Depth (L/D) ratio approximating 14.0 to satisfy <u>estimated</u> longitudinal strength criteria. This geometric ratio was recognized as an approximate measure of longitudinal hull girder stiffness (vertical bending) for bulk-cargo vessels up to 350 feet in length, and this continued to be acceptable to Ship Classification Societies when applied in conjunction with empirical data resources.

A Tribute to our Shipbuilders

As we commemorate the S.S. Edmund Fitzgerald laker, some may also recall the wartime achievement of building over 5,400 merchant ships as the Arsenal of Democracy.

With labor-intensive national composition, about 65% of the production workforce was dominated by ten (10) critical skills. namely:

1. Shipfitters
2. Riggers
3. Loftsman
4. Welders and Burners
5. Machinists
6. Electricians
7. Pipefitters
8. Sheetmetal Workers
9. Boilermakers
10. Electronic Mechanics

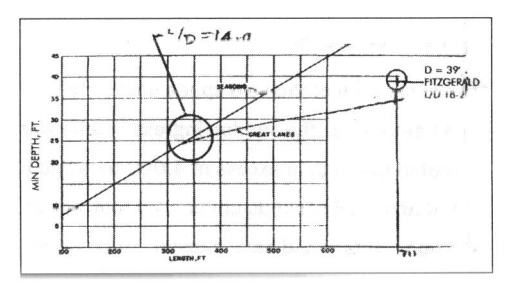

Ratio L/D for Seagoing and Great Lakes ships
The L/D Ratio Is a Rough Measure of Hull Stiffness

A GENERAL VIEW

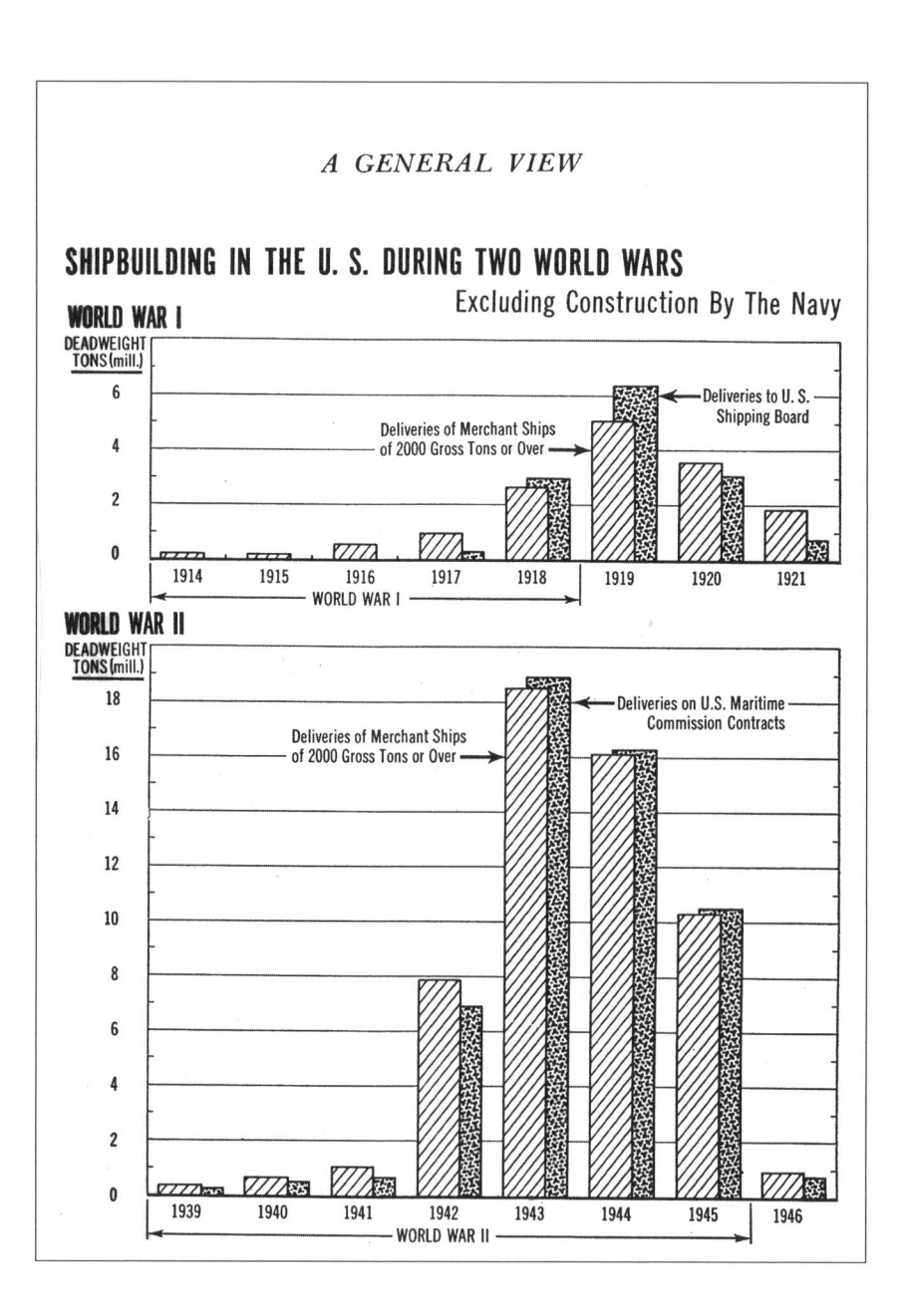

SHIPBUILDING IN THE U. S. DURING TWO WORLD WARS
Excluding Construction By The Navy

WORLD WAR I

Deliveries of Merchant Ships of 2000 Gross Tons or Over

Deliveries to U. S. Shipping Board

WORLD WAR II

Deliveries of Merchant Ships of 2000 Gross Tons or Over

Deliveries on U.S. Maritime Commission Contracts

Midship Section of Typical Great Lakes bulk carrier (Fitzgerald-Type)

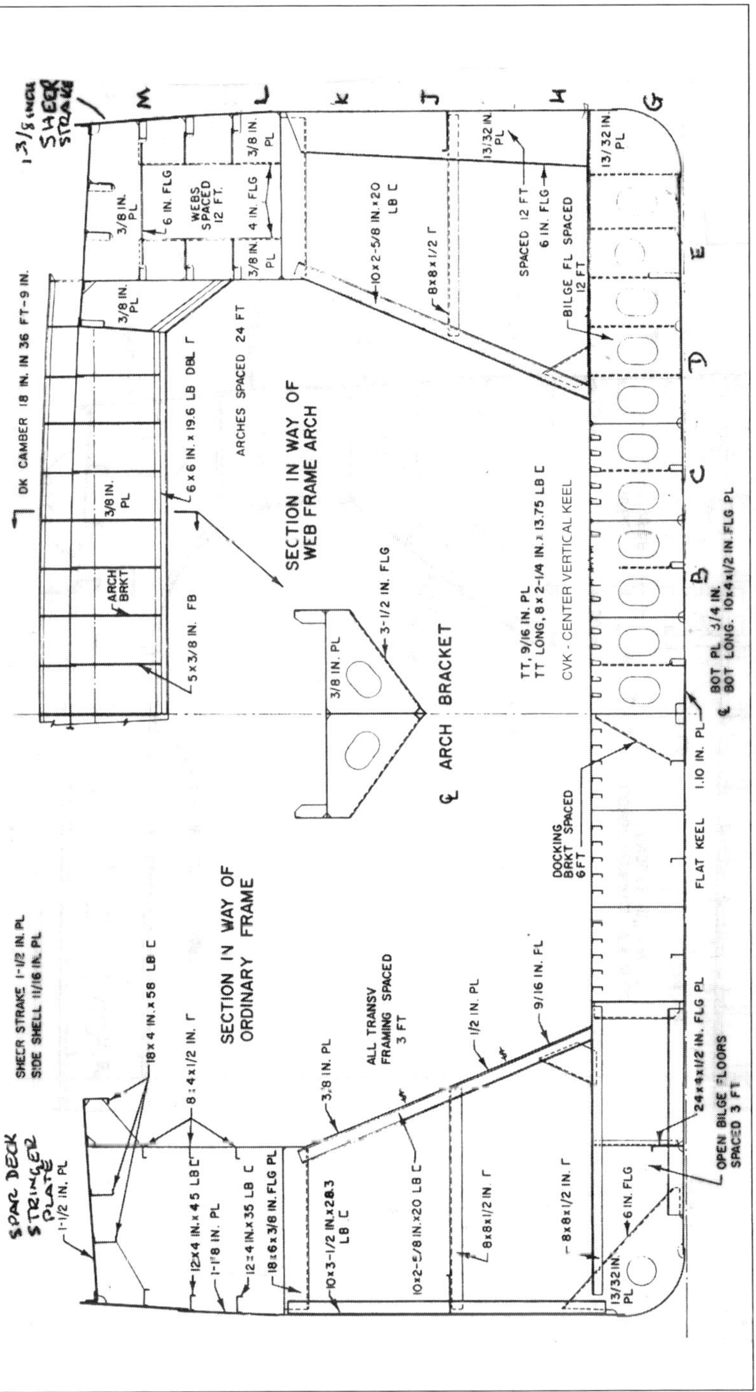

It is worthy of note that the "Fitzgerald" design development assumptions of the early 1950's predated the promulgation of American Bureau of Shipping (ABS) "Rules (Standards) For Building and Classing Bulk Carriers for Service on the Great Lakes. They were not published until 1966 for vessels of 400 to 850 feet in length.

And, needless to say, computer usage, iconic modeling, and finite element analysis were "blue-sky thinking" and in their infancy.

Comprehensive structural strength simulations were also necessarily far from technological reality and, at that time were reliant on parametric study estimations, heuristic reasoning (rules of thumb), Laker designer judgment, and customer preference.

Over the years, Laker designs have adhered to an austere hull "form-follows-function" precept conducive to maximizing transportation of various bulk cargoes at the least cost per ton-mile over a considerable life cycle, while having dimensional compatibility with the prevailing overhead, depth and breadth clearance prerequisites of locks and water channels along their routes.

In the design process, Fitzgerald and other Lakers of that era tended to mainly "grow" in their length dimension for St. Lawrence Seaway utilization compatibility. This hull design "straight jacket" resulted in the Seaway-compatible "Fitzgerald" of the 1950's with a hull length of 729 feet, and an L/D slenderness ratio of 18.2 accompanied by an *unwelcome* hull structural amplification of multi-axial "bending and springing" flexibility.

- 9.0 -
THE 1930'S COMMISSION

Until the mid-1930's, lake vessels and their casualty rates received scant regulatory body oversight until a Special Commission was formed to draft regulations for Great Lakes vessels that spent a lifetime within land-locked maritime transportation systems.

In retrospect, the Commission appears to have erroneously perceived that the operating environment was a generally placid inland waterway, something like the German Rhineland having shallow-draft motorized barges with an L/D ratio of about 30!!

Casualty historians may agree or disagree with some or all of the Commission's conclusions and recommendations, which subsequently preceded introduction of Laker design and construction regulatory oversight, by the United States Coast Guard (USCG), supported by the American Bureau of Shipping (ABS).

The Commission basically concluded that:
1. Laker vessel hulls suffer <u>less</u> apparent damage because of shorter waves, while experiencing <u>long</u> life in a corrosion-free fresh water environment.
2. Distances between terminals are comparatively <u>short</u> and vessels caught in bad weather are seldom without a place to shelter.
3. Bulk-cargo carriers mainly operate in Eastern lakes where weather conditions are more <u>favorable</u>.
4. A <u>lesser</u> longitudinal hull bending strength standard (<u>about 50% of an oceangoing bulker</u>) could be allowable.

In the early-1950's, when there was an absence of <u>directly-applicable</u> ABS Rules for Great Lakes vessels, the Commission's conclusions were apparently considered as sufficiently authoritative guidance, even when developing the Fitzgerald's preliminary hull design, which featured advancements including but not limited to:

> - A significant increase in hull length (729) feet and a (weakening) slenderness/hull stiffness ratio (L/D 18.2) over that used for 600-foot Laker developments during the previous thirty-five (35) years.
> - A radical increase in Westinghouse Electric steam turbine propulsion plant power to 7,500 shaft horsepower with reserve capability to produce a continuous maximum output of 8,200...and requiring a corresponding increase in hull strength compatible with increased thrust and frequency of bow wave encounters.
> - A minimum service speed of 16.3 miles per hour.
> - A three-hold cargo capacity of 860,000 cubic feet and an *original* cargo deadweight exceeding 26,000 tons at the initially assigned midsummer freeboard of 11' 10-3/4."

In stark contrast, motorized <u>Rhineland barges</u> operating in sheltered waters have an <u>L/D Ratio exceeding 30!!</u>

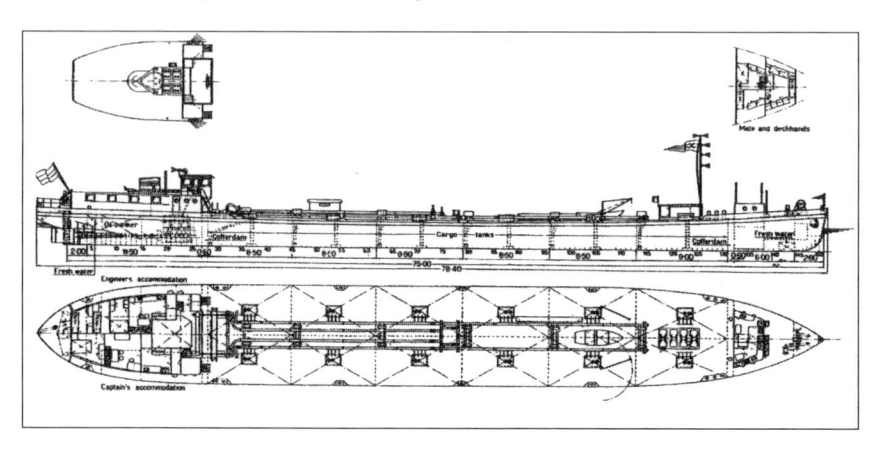

Motor Rhine barge: Principal dimensions

Length o.a . . . . .78.40 m
Length b.p . . . . .75.00 m
Breadth extreme . . . . .9.69 m
Breadth moulded . . . . . . .9.60 m
Depth moulded. . . . . .2.50 m
Draught. . . . . .2.22 m

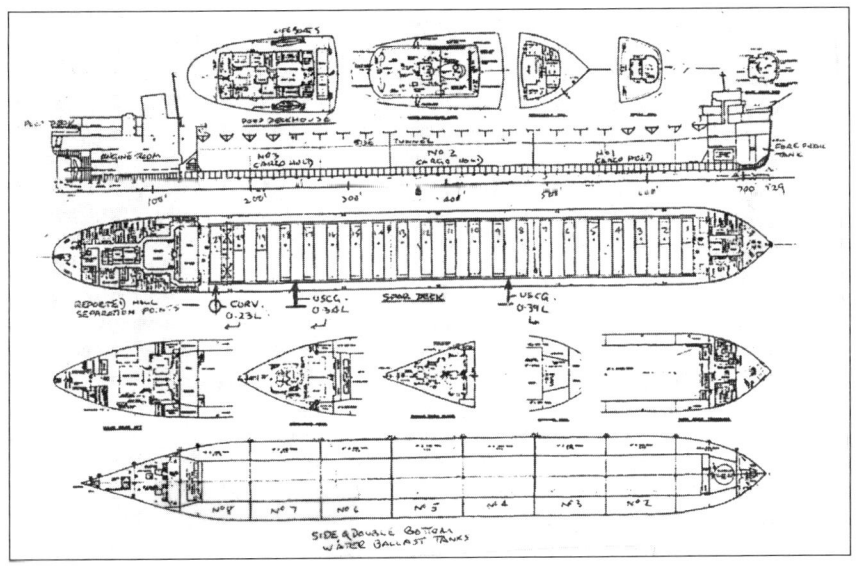

*Edmund Fitzgerald November 10th, 1975
(estimated hull separation points)*
Image from Author's Collection

All of which placed higher multi-axial stress demands on Fitzgerald's full-lined hull structure when driven hard...*as was the case*.

With 20/20 hindsight, the Commission's findings and conclusions appear to have had questionable validity in light of unfavorable past, current and future casualty evidence and accompanying mariner fatalities.

- 10.0 -
NEEDED STRUCTURAL MODIFICATIONS

The hull limberness susceptibility of Fitzgerald and other Lakers may have been partly attributable to the Commission's (flawed) perspective on Great Lakes operations, especially after later USCG Load Line amendments permitted reductions in the minimum freeboard (to increase loaded draft and cargo-carrying capacity) required by CFR Part 45 in the late 1960's.
CIT OP: NTSB Report No.-Mar-78-3

"Freeboard on the Fitzgerald was the distance from the maximum draft permitted to the (Spar) deck at side. A comparison of the requirements for Great Lakes cargo vessels and those vessels operating on the oceans shows that for vessels of similar dimensions, the freeboard required for a Great lakes Load Line and that required for ocean service would be approximately the same. However, the longitudinal strength requirement for a Great Lakes vessel is approximately one-half (1/2) that required for vessels in ocean service."

The author has always viewed with concern the Commission's misperception of the Great Lakes as sheltered waters, the reduced longitudinal strength requirements for Laker structural design, and the USCG Load Line amendment (1969-1973) that authorized reduced freeboard criteria enabling the Fitzgerald to haul about 4,000 additional tons of taconite pellet cargo...*without the design or installation of reinforcing hull structure, or increases in inspection and maintenance requirements.*

Continuance of traditional rule-of-thumb structural design criteria extrapolations (for Fitzgerald) from semi-empirical design standards (used for aging, lesser-powered, 600-footers) appears to have been a risky undertaking *without* significant investments in Research, Development, Test and Evaluation (RDT&E) supplemented by "build and bust" experimentation, and iconic modeling. Albeit, such an approach in the early 1950's would have been anathema to prevailing mindsets by placing Laker designers in decisional situations of "Not knowing what they didn't know", when unaware of today's computerized analytic technologies which could have enabled stress analysis simulations and "red-flagged" excessive hull flexing with multi-axial hull consequences.

One significant empirical reasoning factor appears to have been disregarded with respect to the long-term empirical history of "long-ship" hull fractures occurring at about one-quarter (0.25L) length from the bow and stern. From a longitudinal hull stressing point of view, Fitzgerald's designers should have recognized that the vertical) shearing forces in a hull generate a maximum value at a vessel's neutral axis and at about 0.25L from the bow or stern.

(i) At an earlier time with this in mind, the Lloyds Ship Classification Society Rules required vessels exceeding six hundred (600) feet in length to have treble riveted seams, in these critical hull locations. However, equivalent structural joint reinforcements were not incorporated in the (welded) counterpart Fitzgerald hull plating, that is considered to have initially fractured at the (extreme stress fiber) spar deck, about 0.25L forward of the stern. At the final point of extremis, the weakened and overloaded Fitzgerald was laboring under elevated boarding-sea loadings and multi-directional storm-induced forces...before succumbing to rapid structural fracture propagation, and (overtaking) stern quartering seas leading to capsizing and torsional tear-away at the stern separation.

(ii) Calculations, based on structural design theory applicable to a uniformly-loaded platform (the hull, consumable supplies, and cargo) supported by a waterborne elastic foundation having two wave crests, would have theoretically yielded the least bending moment (BM) and maximum shear forces (SF) at 0.207 L from each end.

(iii) Surveys of the Fitzgerald wreck site, using side-scan sonar and underwater photography showed slight (within range) variance in the hull fracture location at 0.23L (CURV), 0.31L (NTSB) and 0.35L (USCG) from the stern extremity.

(iv) The Great Lakes Shipwreck Historical Museum, at Whitefish

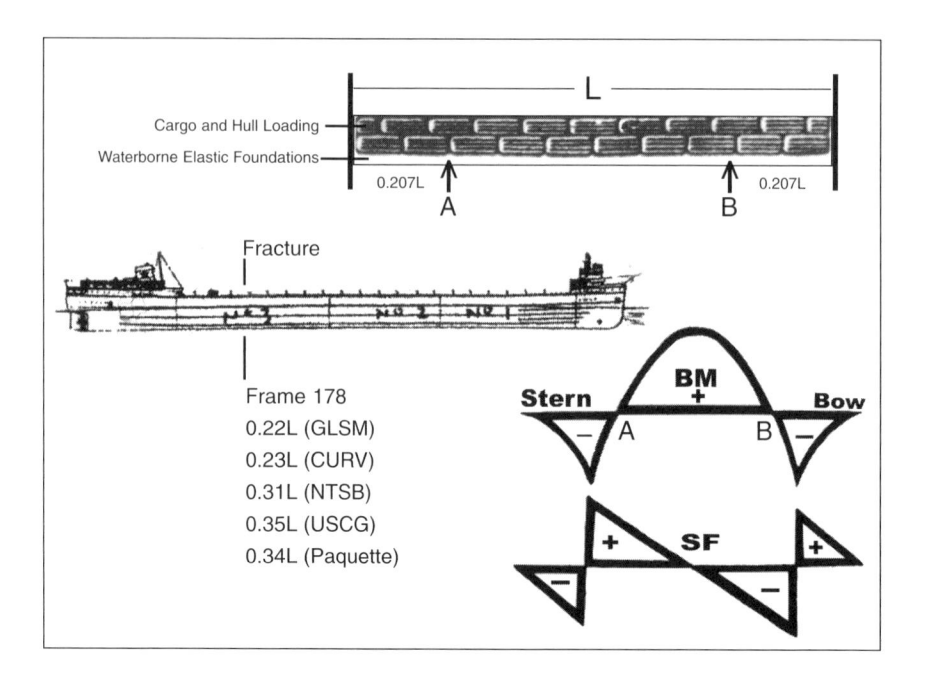

Point, Michigan recently provided compelling side-scan sonar imaging showing hull separation at Frame 178 (0.22L).

(v) Captain Dudley J. Parquette, an experienced Laker mariner stated in his book "The Night The Fitz Went down" (pp.7) that quote "He heard McSorley report hull damage, by saying he was taking water in the No. 7 ballast tank"...which is on the starboard side where the initial asymmetric overloading from astern quartering waves and hull fracturing would have occurred (and induced a listing condition under torsional loading).

Fitzgerald's deteriorating list generated by these astern quartering wave loadings had a speed of advance greater than Fitzgerald. This should be given recognition as a significant factor in the sinking...with cross coupling to structural exacerbation of rapid hull fracture progression in the stern separation/("hinge point") region, as validated by underwater surveys, and in consonance with Captain Paquette's subjective opinion that "long-ship hull failure may be expected to occur at about two-thirds of a ship length from the bow (i.e. 0.34L from the stern)."

In essence, the foregoing evidentiary framework is considered to provide a theoretical and practical preponderance of evidence beyond a reasonable doubt, to <u>counter</u> any assertions that the Fitzgerald loss was attributable to mariner navigational incompetence or ship handling that fatally resulted in shoaling. (i.e. <u>The Fitzgerald's demise was considered by CRA to be for reasons other than shoaling</u>). And with most likely probable cause being major hull structural fracture at Frame No. 178 (in the expected 0.25L region for "long-ships")

Captain Dudley J. Paquette of the S.S. Wilfred Sikes

Other evidence points of notable consideration are germane but not limited to:

(a) The shortcomings of (1950's) initial structural design driven by technical extrapolations made in the absence of <u>directly applicable</u> American Bureau of Shipping (ABS) Rules For Building and Classing Bulk Carriers For Service on the Great Lakes, when coupled with the limitations of extant merchant shipbuilding technology.

(b) An inadequate conventional Great Lakes shipyard and shipowner approach to the requirements and procedures for design and construction of an advanced Laker vessel without dimensional or powering precedent, or consideration of Research, Test and Evaluation (RDT&E) principles.

(c) An austere ship acquisition policy, minimizing expenditures considered subordinate to actual vessel construction.

(d) Questionable production quality control standards for welders and their training, and the receipt inspection of hull construction materials having highly-variable physical, mechanical, and chemical properties.

- 10.1 -
INCREASED CARGO LOADING

Re: Need For Post-Delivery Hull Strengthening.

The USCG Load Line authorization (1969-1973) enabled the Fitzgerald to earn increased revenue by hauling approximately 4,000 additional tons of iron ore per trip when operating at a deeper draft. This increased cargo loading was about 15% above the specified cargo-carrying capability of the original structural design, and there was NO evidence that additional reinforcement was ever designed or installed to withstand this superimposed deeper-draft cargo loading.

Further, an appropriate increase in the original midship section structural modulus calculation, concomitant with a deeper Winter draft was absent. No USCG or ABS review and approval, could be identified.

And, based on Final Departure Drafts, the Fitzgerald was proceeding at the Authorized Deeper (Winter) Draft, in a Hogged (Hull Bending Upward) in an overloaded condition at the time of sinking.

At the onset of Hull Fracturing, the Fitzgerald's Longitudinal Bending Strength was estimated to be about 11% Deficient).

- 10.2 -
NEED FOR CARGO HATCH COVER AND COAMING STRENGTHENING

Re: Increased water-head loading commensurate with freeboard reductions, enabling deeper boarding seas.

The Fitz's twenty-one (21) steel cargo hatch covers and supporting peripheral coamings were originally designed in compliance with regulatory weather-tight criteria requiring structural suitability for a water-head loading of 4'-0" during heavy weather conditions.

Cargo hatch covers were not structurally upgraded to sustain an additional 3' 3-1/4" water-head loading commensurate with the authorized deeper winter draft.

Cit Op.-NTSB Report No. MR-78-3.

"The NTSB Assigned Probable Cause Justifications Which Included "The Hydrostatic And Hydrodynamic Forces Imposed On The Hatch Covers By Heavy Boarding Seas At The Reduced Freeboard And With The Increasing List Condition Caused (Certain) Hatch Covers To Collapse." Thus confirming the Author's prognosis.

Subsequent NTSB testing and analysis confirmed that boarding seas could have induced sufficient stresses to cause the catastrophic (buckling) failure of one or more of the hatch covers when the Fitzgerald was overwhelmed by abnormal boarding waves.

The author's book "For Whom The Bells Toll" corroborated the results, and further highlighted the fact that the high-density taconite pellets occupied only about 50% of the cargo hold lower volume (with about 50% of upper cargo-hold volume void). It was estimated that water ingress through one (1) breached spar deck opening *(48ft x 11ft)* could have flooded a cargo hold in about fourteen (14) seconds when (short and steep) boarding waves were at least of 20 feet height.

The covers were each of about 10,000# weight and fabricated from 5/16" thick stiffened steel. Each cover was secured by sixty-eight (68) pivoting and adjustable Kestner clamps, arranged with approximately two (2) feet spacing around their perimeters having 9/16 inch thick rubber gaskets. Exposed hatch cover perimeter surfaces had concave "button" recesses on which downward adjustable clamping forces were exerted to satisfy *"weather-tightness"* (versus water-tightness) testing requirements.

It should be recognized that only *"weather"* tightness was required (46 CFR 42.09-40), for the original cover design. This had lesser water spray force consideration than that commensurate with increased immersion and pressure under prolonged submergence...having dynamically transient hydrostatic and hydrodynamic force awash conditions at the reduced freeboard (deeper draft).

With Hatch Covers
(54'0" x 11'7")
Image from Author's Collection

Cargo Hatch Openings (21)
(48'0" x 11'0")
and Kestner Clamps
(68 per hatch)
(1428 per shipset)
Image from Author's Collection

For Human Endurance Reasons there Is Evidence Revealing <u>Laxity</u> In The Repetitive And Laborious "Real-World" Shipboard Securing Of Kestner Clamps (1,428) Under Exposed Weather Conditions, and Prior To Each Voyage Departure.

Ineffective weather tight closures are grounds for denying issuance of a Load Line Certificate Of Inspection.

ECONOMIC FACTORS

Weekend work would not be done if it would necessitate the payment of overtime rates. Hatch cover positioning operations (requiring on-board electric crane support and Kestner clamp securing) would be deferred until the following day if overtime payment was not authorized.

More (but not all) clamps were usually secured during 8-hour weekdays when overtime payments were not expected.

Whenever clamping was incomplete on some hatch covers prior to departure, each hatch cover was usually partly secured with only two clamps at each corner and one centered at the front, rear and outboard edges. (A total of twelve (12) out of a total of 68 per hatch cover). While underway with favorable conditions, incompletely clamped hatch covers would be secured.

It is notable that the USCG did take affirmative action, by <u>rescinding</u> the (1973) Load Line Regulation amendment permitting reduced freeboard (deeper draft) loadings, and carrying out ex post-facto hydrostatic pressure testing of cargo hatch covers.

Fitzgerald and fleet-wide modification of hatch covers and coamings was <u>never ordered</u> by the USCG or shipowner and this was probably due to potential cost impact and revenue losses due to interrupted cargo deliveries...although this non-modification decision was reportedly predicated on the supposedly trouble-free performance of other Laker vessels having similar hatch opening closure systems.

PRACTICAL FACTORS

Poorly maintained Kestner clamps could be inoperable or loose.

Reduced-size crew complacency, monotonous repetivity, and human endurance could impair expectancy of fully securing (1,428) clamps on each and every (5)-day cycle under heavy weather and winter conditions.

Unloading in Toledo, Ohio - using Hulett Bucket system
Image Courtesy of Marine Historical Society of Detroit

Cargo unloading operations using Hulett Bucket system
Images Courtesy of Marine Historical Society of Detroit

Hulett Unloader Clamshell-Type Bucket
Images Courtesy of Marine Historical Society of Detroit

Unloading with Gantry Crane system
Image Courtesy of Marine Historical Society of Detroit

A typical bulker offload

1. A bulldozer is loaded into the hold.	2. The bulldozer pushes cargo to the center of the hold.	3. The gantry crane picks up the cargo.	4. The gantry crane removes the cargo from the ship.	5. The gantry crane moves the cargo to a bin on the pier.

Photos courtesy of Danny Cornelissen of porpictures.nl.

- 11.0 -
HINDSIGHT PERSPECTIVES
- 11.1 -
PUBLIC HEARING DILEMMAS

It is general knowledge that the official NTSB and USCG public hearing reports have proven to be analytically incomplete & <u>inconclusive</u> and this is (at least) mainly due to:

(i) The hearing scope of inquiry duration, imposed by the USCG Marine Board Chairman, that resulted in an unrealistically short time-frame (only) extending from the Fitzgerald's date of departure (November 9th 1975) from the Burlington Northern ore-loading docks at Superior, Wisconsin, to the time of sinking at about 1915 e.s.t. on November 10th 1975.

The public hearing was convened at the USCG Ninth District Headquarters in Cleveland, Ohio on November 18th 1975.

At that time, there appeared to be a lack of Board awareness that the Fitzgerald was reputed to have a significant number of critical (*unrepaired*) hull welding deficiencies throughout her history, that may (or may-not) be documented in the public record, and did require full disclosure.

Determinations and findings contributory to probable cause conclusions by the Board, for the Fitzgerald sinking casualty, were <u>not</u> considered feasible (by CRA et al) in the absence of a comprehensive understanding of the vessel's material condition during operations prior to, and inclusive of, the hearing scope duration directed by the Chairman.

These factors were also exacerbated by:

(i) An apparent lack of technical sensitivity toward the deleterious structural damage on safe vessel operations, caused by the destructive impacts on cargo-hold and other hull structure caused by Hulett and Brownhoist bucket clamshell unloaders at dockside; and inadequate panelist familiarity with Fitzgerald's (1950') genetic design origins; and her questionable life-cycle maintenance and repair history.

(ii) Conflicting and inconsistent witness testimony concerning Fitzgerald's and Anderson's navigational course(s), and in-transit speed(s) as reportedly used in Captain McSorley's dead-reckoning communications, were dubious Radar inoperability and vessel safety relative to the navigation of both vessels near (unchartered) shoaling areas and "saltie" vessels in transit, were also subject to questioning.

(iii) Disparity and questionable accuracy of statements made by the S.S. Anderson's late Master (Captain "Bernie" Cooper), <u>with corroboration by his crew cadre,</u> during initial under-oath testimony to the USCG Marine Board panelists became self evident.

Subsequent to Captain Cooper giving key (under-oath) testimony before the Board, they were made aware of a taped and contradictory telecon which Captain Cooper made with (Anderson's) corporate officials at the U.S. Steel Corporation and the Oglebay Norton Company on November 11th 1975...*less than twenty-four (24) hours after the Fitzgerald sinking.*

Regrettably, Captain Cooper undermined his credibility when he kept asking his organizational superiors the questions "What do you want me to say?"...even though he was an eyewitness to events and <u>had already</u> provided testimony under oath.

It is recalled that this procedural anomaly occurred subsequent to the late Captain "Bernie" Cooper and crew members of the U.S. Steel Corporation's Anderson (then-operated by their Pittsburgh Steamship Division), *initially* provided under-oath testimony that "Fitzgerald <u>was closer to the shoal than they would have wanted to</u> be."

It should not be forgotten that these (Anderson) mariners, were the sole eye-witnesses responsible for providing directional communication to compensate for Fitzgerald's <u>inoperable</u> radar and other navigational aids under reportedly severe snowstorm conditions, and that they subsequently affirmed that "The Fitzgerald was <u>not near</u> the shoal," when officially providing (under oath) testimony to the Board. (Albeit, snow and high-wave storm conditions may have impaired the accuracy of Anderson's radar signal (scatter) definition, and her track variations were weather-compliant and therefore of questionable credibility for official record tracking purposes).

In retrospect, they <u>never</u> made an affirmative statement that a damaging shoal <u>encounter</u> had been physically witnessed, or relatively logged or <u>plotted</u> on (Anderson) charts.

This undermined the Author's confidence in statements by Anderson's crew eye-witnesses and others in their chain of command who appeared to be complicit in a cover-up strategy to avoid perceived liability claims.

The Board was advised that "each Master is expected to use his experience to evaluate the most current and accurate weather information in deciding the best course of action for the safety of his ship." Both ships, Arthur M. Anderson and the Edmund Fitzgerald were official weather reporting vessels. (Ergo: McSorley's judgment should have been given trustworthy precedence over conflicting shoaling proximity statements provided on tape by Captain Cooper and his pilothouse officers.)

> As minimum, this situation led to an <u>inability</u> to ascertain:
> (a) Whether or not the Anderson (<u>unknowingly</u>) gave erroneous directional guidance causing Fitzgerald to transit over <u>unchartered</u> shoaling area(s), and also misrepresented the safety and frequency of other vessels transitting to or from Whitefish Bay.
> (b) An <u>inability</u> of USCG and NTSB panelists to reconstruct variable Fitzgerald and Anderson track lines, time fixes...and

corresponding transit speeds, which they estimated to range from 5 mph to 66 mph (a physical impossibility for Lakers). and involving:

(iv) Non-disclosure or explanation for the covert excising of two (2) voyage pages from Anderson's log book and whether (or not) remaining entries were reconstructed by expost facto memory consensus and after considerable hiatus.

(v) Uncertainty about the operating condition of Fitzgerald's dual radar system, communication and power supply equipment, navigational aids and the incompleteness of inter-vessel dialogue.

- 11.2 -
CARGO LOADING AND TRANSPORTATION

Fitzgerald completed her cargo load-out at Burlington Northern Railroad Dock No. 1 November 9th 1975 at 1415 hrs. This pier, known as "chute pier" was equipped with built-in storage bins known as "pockets" which were usually filled before a vessel arrived.

Chutes were lowered from each "pocket" to direct the flow into the hatches of the vessel. Most of the pockets had 300 tons of taconite pellets; however, a few pockets that were filled with 100 tons or 200 tons.

Typical Ore Loading Dock
Image from Author's Collection

During the 1975 season, Fitzgerald had (only) loaded at the Burlington dock on two other trips and would have usually loaded at the Reserve Mining Company dock at Silver Bay, Minnesota where two conveyor belts are used for load-out. No explanation was given for the cargo loading diversion.

The Chief Mate, Mr. John H. McCarthy informed dock personnel the vessel's final drafts were 27 feet 2 inches forward and 27 feet 6 inches aft., giving a mean draft of 27 feet 4 inches. This corresponded to a freeboard of 11 feet 8 inches.

The Chief Mate had been employed by the vessel's operator since 1947 in various capacities, including relief master in 1966 and 1971, and had served aboard the Fitzgerald as Chief Mate since April 1975.

Since no midship draft was recorded the amount of stationary hull prestressing deflective hogging (hull bending upward) computed to 2 inches...based on Fitzgerald's authorization to load with a Winter freeboard of 11 feet 6 inches per amended 1973 USCG Load Line Regulations.

A former Chief Mate who served on Fitzgerald during the 1973-1974 seasons testified that he had never seen the loading manual and he relied on the Chief Mate's notebook for loading information. In doing so, he confirmed denial of the Author's (1958) request to prepare such a manual prior to vessel delivery.

The USCG Marine Board Report states that "Final Cargo adjustments are made to achieve *no hog*, however, one inch of sag or "belly" is considered acceptable and an even keel is most desirable."

Bow and stern drafts were taken after reported receipt of approximately 26,118 long tons of taconite pellets and 50,013 gallons of No. 6 fuel oil delivered by barge.

It should be recognized that 26,118 long tons of high-density taconite pellets is estimated to only require about 417,856 cubic feet (about 49%) of cargo-hold volume, whereas a total of 860,950 cubic feet was actually available. Thereby allowing the Chief Mate to have considerable latitude in the physical distribution of taconite and some other bulk cargoes, in the absence of a loading manual.

By reviewing available cargo-hold capacities of No. 1 @ 309,942, No. 2 @ 241,066, and No. 3 @ 309, 942 cubic feet, it can be seen that any two (2) (of the three (3), cargo holds had adequate volumetric capacity for stowage of 26,118 long tons (417,856 cubic feet) of taconite pellets.

- 11.3 -
POTENTIAL (OTHER) SHIPMENTS (NATIONAL SECURITY)

While it is highly desirable to have uniform longitudinal and vertical loading for minimized stress and vibration, throughout the hull structure, it would appear that there is ample latitude to physically distribute and transport taconite pellets segregated from security-sensitive, and non-conventional, cargoes without compromising measured drafts required for lock and limited water channel depths navigation.

With this as forethought, the Oglebay Norton Company as a national asset in Great Lakes shipping and the mining of ore, aggregates, sand, gravel and other earth-originated bulk commodities (including uranium which was believed to be scarce in the early 1970's), may have directed its Columbia Transport Division to authorize special loading arrangements at the Burlington facility with unloading at Zug Island, Michigan on an urgent, high security case bases with special cargo stowage, shipment and handling aboard Fitzgerald by temporarily expanded specialized crew.

Under such "special arrangements" it would be understandable why discussion and wreckage site investigation is (still) discouraged thirty-three (33) years after Fitzgerald's sinking. During the Cold War period, The United States Department of Energy (DOE) played a vital role in national defense, and was actively engaged in the buildup of strategic and critical materials, including the acquisition of uranium reserve assets having acceptable U_{308} concentrates.

High-purity uranium can be prepared by various thermal decomposition and electrolytic processes, requiring industrial support from specialized industrial activities that operated in the downriver Detroit region. With DOE sponsorship, and trustworthy private contractor cooperation, it would seem valid to anticipate that it would have certainly been in the national interest to maintain controlled shipment security for the minimizing of public risk.

Under these circumstances it would have appeared prudent to utilize waterborne point-to-point (Superior, Wisconsin to Zug Island, Michigan) Laker transportation...versus countering the operational hazards of wheeled vehicles and shipment detractors on commercial railroads and highways, when traveling through highly-populated areas, while on the final lap to security-sensitive research and processing facilities having diversified industrial interests...such as steel making, synthetics, chemicals, etc.

While such a thesis (by CRA) is only supported by limited corroborating evidence; in Cold-War retrospect it does appear to have merit...and could provide partial explanation of the informational obstruction (gag orders), incommunicado positions, and Canadian restrictions applicable to the sensitive Fitzgerald wreckage site access by divers, salvors, et al.

Based on our research experience it may or may-not be plausible that some, or many, of involved parties are able to furnish constructive information on the Fitzgerald's final cargo manifest and possible vulnerability to a rarely-discussed explosion...and considering the reported witness sighting(s) of <u>an instantaneous*bright flash.</u>

The following tabular summary shows a percentile distribution of probable loss causes for <u>oceangoing</u> bulkers, based on interpretation of data accumulated over a broadened time spectrum and made available from various credible sources.

Attributable Causes	**1960-1994**	**1990-1994**
Possible Hull Damage	29.9%	28.6%
Wrecked or Stranded	28.3	24.1
*Fire and/or explosion	18.6	20.5
Collision	9.6	8.9
Missing unexplained	5.2	9.8
Machinery damage	3.9	3.6
Engine room flooding	3.4	4.5
Cargo shifting	1.1	-

- 11.4 -
POTENTIAL (OTHER) SHIPMENTS (HIGHER VALUE MINERALS)

On the other hand, with less-clandestine objectives, corporate executives may have been exploring (unidentified) higher-value cargo transportation opportunities from mineral-rich natural and processed resources...to enhance Laker revenues.

It is known that USA/Canada northern regions have considerable natural mineral resources which require special mining and transportation safety precautions for workers and their equipment. The higher-value rock deposit resources, such as iron, coal, bauxite and others are dense and can have corrosive and abrasive effects. They usually also contain entrained moisture and pyritic wastes that are conducive to spontaneous combustion during shipment.

The 1960 Safety Of Life At Sea (SOLAS) Convention sought to control this underway shipboard problem, by requiring that such spaces be ventilated, and the cargo to be leveled, or trimmed. Excavators and/or bulldozers are used in the cargo holds to reduce the amount of cargo in contact with air and the liberation of gasses susceptible to spontaneous combustion, or explosion by an ignition source.

If a cargo hold is full, a technique called "tomming" is used which involves excavating a six (6) feet-deep hole below a hatch cover and filling it with bagged cargo or weights.

It is not known whether Fitzgerald received additional cargo hold ventilation or gas-monitoring capability, or if special on-board precautions were taken to prevent conditions of spontaneous combustion preceding an explosion related to witnesses claiming instantaneous sighting(s) of bright flash.

- 11.5 -
AUTHOR'S FOR THE RECORD EXPLOSION COMPARISON WITH S.S. CARL D. BRADLEY SINKING:

Ref: USCG Marine Board of Investigation Report (a-9 Bd) dtd July 7 1959.

It was recognized that during the (1958) sinking of SS Carl D. Bradley (Official No. 2267776), the German oceangoing vessel M/V Cristian Santori reported "*A flash of flame*" and concluded that the Bradley had exploded.

The Board noted that "This observation and that of (two) survivors reporting the eruption of steam, *bright flames* and smoke, had occurred after the vessel was parted (and sinking), and opined (page 12) that water rushing into combustion chambers of the boilers was the cause, after the stern section plunged amid an eruption of steam and combustible materials."

The Board also opined that:
"The Bradley hull fractured (during hogging) and could have proceeded on course for about <u>one mile</u> before eventually breaking in half, and (within three minutes):"

- "The stern sagged and the in-ballasted condition vessel heaved upward (hogged) before parting and having the stern section settle from the forward end on an even keel, then plunged (still on an even keel) with the stern counter going down last."
- "The bow swung to port, remaining on an even keel and the after end (of the bow section) swung to starboard, before settling on an even keel, and finally listing to port prior to rollover and sinking."

While the Bradley's hull sinking dynamics may bear some resemblance to that of Fitzgerald, and the "*flash of flame*" observations may stimulate common thoughts of explosion(s) originating in submerging combustion chambers of the propulsion plant steam boilers, the Author does consider other reserved opinion (for Fitzgerald) to be appropriate in that the Fitzgerald cargo-hold devastation region was longitudinally <u>dispersed</u> over about two hundred (200) feet and the Bradley hull structural fracture was <u>concentrated</u> at about amidships without explosive characteristics at that location.

However, a subjective casualty reconstruction comparison should not prelude the probability of contained (Fitzgerald) boiler explosion upon immersion, causing propulsion plant shutdown, and visible flame expulsions via the smoke stack (funnel) prior to inversion of the stern hull section.

- 12.0 -
HULL DESTRUCTION DIORAMAS

The lake floor "still-life" diorama reconstruction, showing Fitzgerald's hull wreckage and partial debris fields are considered to have technical credibility and historical merit, in that extensive use was made of USCG video tapes from remote vehicle investigations followed by experienced pairing of underwater photographs with line drawings and various official survey documents.

For full effect, the diorama should also be visualized during incremental structural decomposition accompanied by forward speed deceleration during hull cargo compartment collapse, cargo-spilling, and the dynamic submergence evolution in a turbulent water column.

The late Mr. Richard W. Sullivan, senior illustrator at Potomac Research Incorporated demurred in making no attempt to arrive at conclusions (from his reconstruction), about the cause of Fitzgerald sinking. However, structural hull failure and internal explosion conclusions appear to have merit when objective and subjective forensic evaluation is applied to the devastated two hundred and thirteen (213) feet "missing" parallel hull region between the upright but dislocated forward hull, and the inverted stern section.

By introspection, various scenarios may be developed, including the following in which it appeared that a powerful explosion could have occurred in Cargo Hold No. 2, at about mid-length of the vessel; causing the partial spar deck to be ejected upward and off-hull before landing alongside an *already-separated* and inverted stern section. (Lemma 10). It is also noted that Mr. Sullivan has modeled No. 11 and No. 12 hatchway openings (at about the mid-length of Cargo Hold No. 2) *without* steel hatch covers and *with* distorted coamings.

The spar deck crane rails facilitate visual orientation, and "artist license" discretion cannot be absolutely eliminated.

The (39-feet deep) outboard shell plating and side framing, for port and starboard hull sides, are not shown, and could have been "blown off" into a (to be located) debris field at about 530-feet depth, by an internal explosion in Cargo-Hold No. 2...as the submerging vessel spilled cargo from the hull-(Lemma 9) break point immediately forward of the dislocated stern module.

The cellular double bottom (CDB) construction is correctly modeled, *without* welded shell plating (a "piranha-like effect" having shell plating joints fail with hydrodynamic "unzipping" of unwelded shell plating from internal CDB structure and is vertically sheared from the inverted stern module...but without variance in orientation (i.e. Upside-down longitudinal alignment same as stern).

Photos below and on the following pages of the Richard Sullivan's diorama model of the S.S. Edmund Fitzgerald used by permission from photographer Scott Monsma.

Mr. Sullivan's model (1999) and paintings of the Fitzgerald are now in the Wisconsin Maritime Museum, Manitowoc, Wisconsin

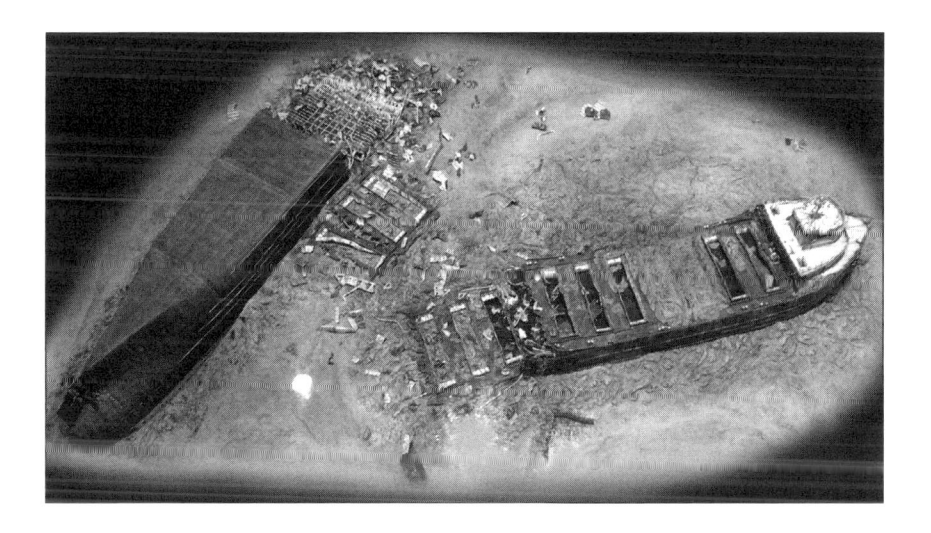

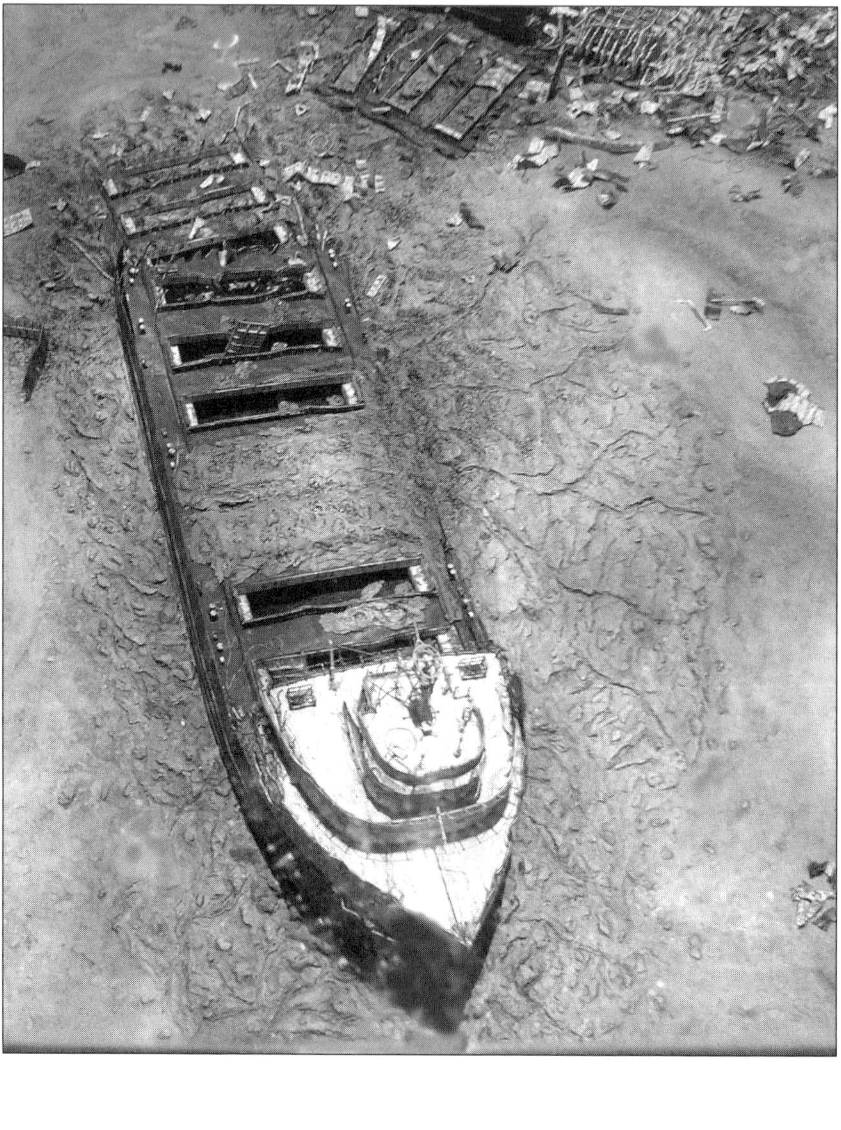

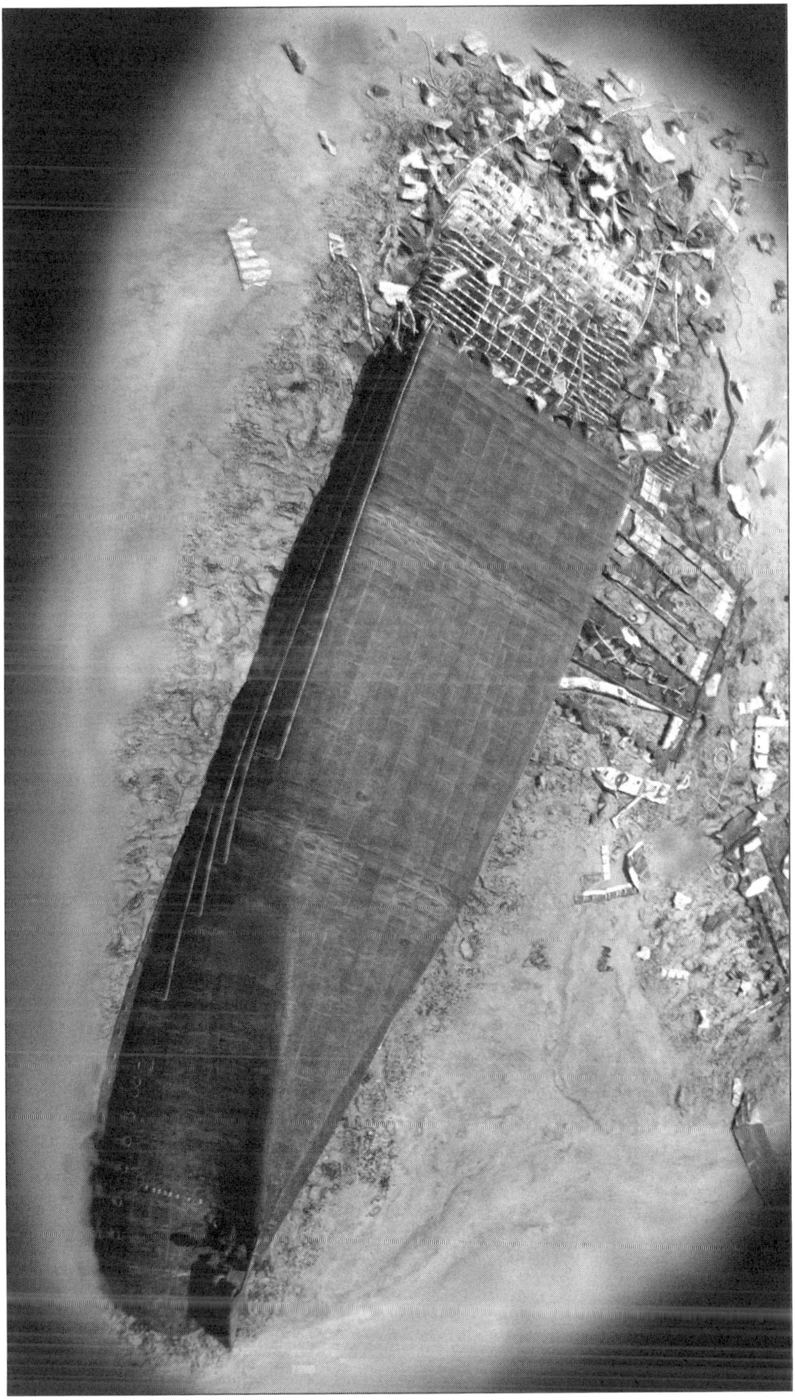

This structural depiction may be attributable to a combination of welded shell-plate joint and steel material failures, with "blowout" from internal explosive force(s).

It is noted that the cellular double bottom (CDB), side-shell plating, and spar deck construction are modeled as attached and contiguous with the dislocated bow section. With stern module separation and free-flow spillages from, for example: Cargo Hold No. 2 (special cargo) and Cargo Hold No. 3 (taconite), the fractured Fitzgerald would have experienced a forward shift in her longitudinal center of gravity which would have induced a bow-down attitude followed by inclined impact with the lake floor. (Lemma 9)

In turn, this would have caused the forward Cargo Hold No. 1 taconite to flow ahead and to act as an explosive force mitigation buffer, allowing the spar deck and some hatch coamings and covers to remain reasonably intact.

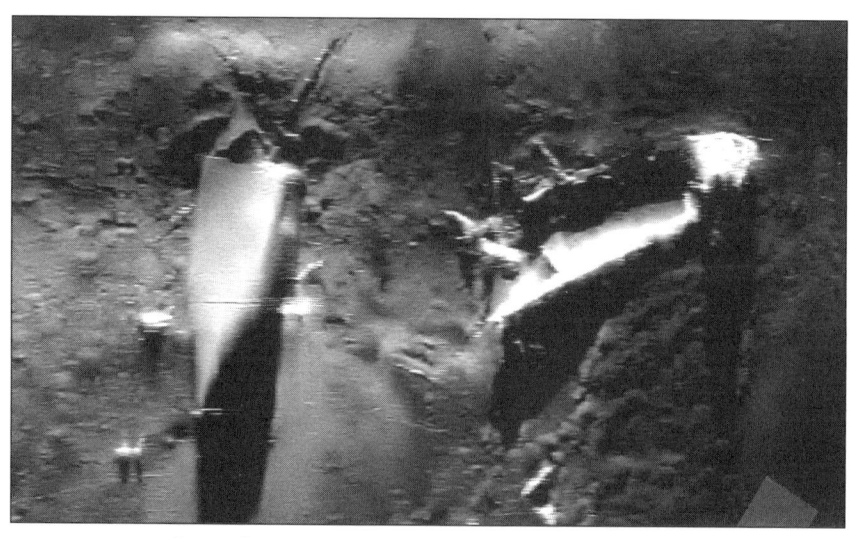

Sonar Imaging of S.S. Fitzgerald at 530-foot Depth
Image Courtesy of: Great Lakes Shipwreck Historical Society (GLSHS), Sault Ste. Marie, Michigan

- 13.0 -
SHOALING (OR NOT)

This potential cause of the Fitzgerald casualty was given considerable review by the United States Coast Guard (USCG) Marine Board, with independent investigation conducted by representatives from the National Transportation Safety Board (NTSB), the Great Lakes shipping industry and privately-sponsored parties.

The USCG and NTSB findings and recommendations therefrom are published in the Federal Register and, if the USCG did not accept some of the NTSB recommendations as the decisional body having primacy the USCG was required to set forth in detail the reasons for such refusal. Cit Op. -NTSB Report No. Mar-78-3.

The NTSB <u>Did Not</u> Assign Probable Cause Justification To <u>Shoaling For Loss Of The S.S. Edmund Fitzgerald</u>, and neither did other experienced mariners highly qualified in the navigational field.

The Author concurs that: Shoaling could not have occured on a destructive scale capable of causing <u>terminal</u> loss of the Fitzgerald, despite photographic and rock-sampling evidence purportedly recovered by agents of the Oglebay Norton Company, seeking affirmation of hull-damaging vessel contact with an underwater topographic obstruction.

It is hypothesized that damaged bottom and/or lower side-shell plating could have become separated from hull structure at other times in a number of locations, allowing and flooding of Cellular Double Bottom (CDB) and side ballast tanks. While the official record states that Captain McSorley had activated ballast pumps, the water ingress evidently exceeded stripping pumping capacity and, in effect, the pumps would have been called upon to empty Lake Superior and not specific ballast tankage...when clear of Superior and Caribou shoal proximities. Immediate outcomes of this ballast tank flooding would have been a gradual reduction in reserve buoyancy, with an increase in asymmetric sinkage, and a listing condition.

Catastrophic capsizing would have been delayed by the hull design compartmentation enabling survivability with any three (3) ballast tanks, on one side of the vessel, to be completely breached.

Whether these be in a recent or distant time frame, it is accepted that the probable causes for most vessel losses remain elusive when occurring without witnesses, survivors or distress signals and without adequate navigation equipment and reliable hydrographic information.

During the hearings, it was determined that the S.S. Edmund Fitzgerald could have been using chart Nos. L.S. 9 and vintage (1919) Canadian Chart 2310, which were confirmed by a CSS Bayfield hydrographic survey to be inaccurate...by failing to show that the northern end of the shoals north of Caribou Island extended approximately one mile further out into Lake Superior than indicated on Canadian chart No. 2310!

This localized area re-survey appeared to be a shoaling "minefield" of navigational uncertainties, which were either used or avoided by experienced mariners who were able to recognize shallowing conditions by the "steepening" of wave heights and their frequency of wave encounter and bow slamming...when "smelling the land."

In an overview, it is highly probable that hydrographers of a previous era probably had budget-constrained surveying priorities, at a time when earlier vessel drafts were of lesser risk to shoaling. Consequently this could have negated a predisposition toward the exercise of a broader work scope, with regard to updating hydrography information of the whole Canadian shoreline lee, from Thunder Bay to Sault Ste. Marie. Albeit shoaling risks would have still been present in the absence of modern navigational and communication equipment.

It may be fairly hypothesized that this whole hydrographic zone would most probably have had extensive shallower shoaling outcroppings (and shipwrecks) in the Canadian land mass littoral zone which would have historically been contributory to an extensive graveyard of trading vessel casualties (of lesser design than Fitzgerald), that may have encountered unmarked submerged obstructions along this sheltered course.

While the CSS Bayfield's re-surveying operation successfully confirmed the Caribou Island and Superior Shoal topographic and geographic extents, it certainly did-not/could-not validate other shoaling conjecture and the inconsistent evidence rendered by Fitzgerald's tracking observers on the Laker S.S. Arthur M. Anderson.

Regrettably, past and present writers and investigators have continued to concentrate on perceived scenarios of shoaling hazards off Caribou Island and some other candidate locations, at the expense of a systemic perspective. All of which had technical dependency on vintage (circa 1919) hydrographic survey charts which were only (in part) resurveyed as part of the USCG's Fitzgerald casualty investigation.

Throughout and following public hearings, the proximity of Fitzgerald's downbound course was subjectively reported as *close* to Caribou Island's enigmatic "6-fathom (36 feet) shoal, and this still-water depth became the focal point for a number of Fitzgerald sinking theories.

The so-called Six-Fathom Shoal extends to the North from Caribou Island (see image on next page).

One theory about the loss of Fitzgerald is that it struck the shoals, was damaged, lost reserve buoyancy and began to take on water that eventually sank the ship.

Additionally, some theories introduced a shoal depth decrement to allow for variable still-water depth reductions potentially caused by vertical seiche oscillatory effects, which were postulated to have had potential for reducing Fitzgerald's below-keel clearance, and facilitated her hull puncturing upon bottom plating impact with this or any other shoal.

With open-minded, unbiased candor, it is conceivable that any vessel using such a poorly charted sheltered coastline course in the subject Canadian littoral under severe storm conditions, and having forces requiring a wheelsman to follow a track of least-damaging resistance, could have encountered incidental underwater navigational hazards in the form of uncharted shoals and shipwrecks. And, although the Board panelists were unable to reconstruct the Anderson and Fitzgerald courses and speeds, it cannot be denied that both vessels were (technically) proceeding with common direction, toward safe harbor at Whitefish Bay, but with correctable course variations to compensate for storm weather forces.

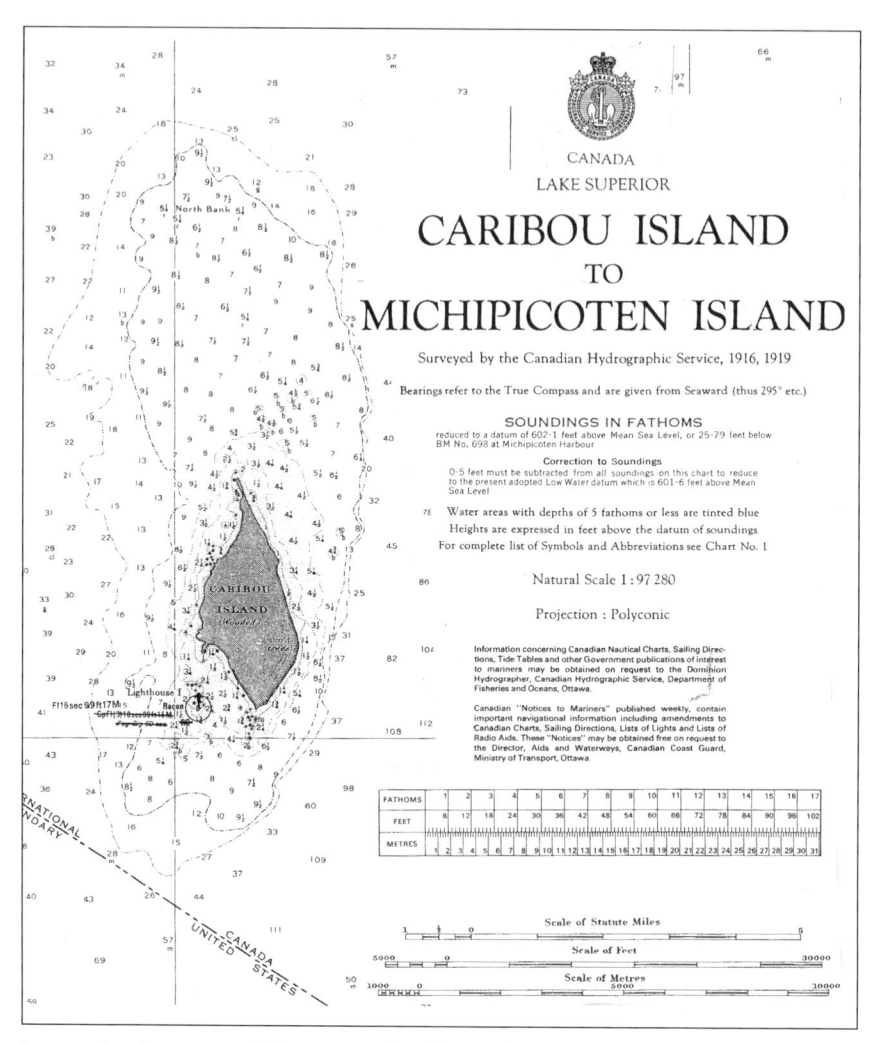

In Contrast To Catastrophic Shoaling

Based on circumstantial evidence, the probable causes of Fitzgerald's loss could, in varying degrees, be attributable to hull structural damage sustained "somewhere in transit", and/or questionable hull maintenance and repair, and a "design too far", contributing to catastrophic systematic failure.

A catastrophic surface breakup of the Fitzgerald's hull would have (almost) completely arrested forward ship motion at the onset of structural fracturing, surface breakup, and submergence with a temporarily attached and "hinged-down" stern section acting as a drogue braking device.

Catastrophic sinking <u>due to shoaling</u> was unequivocally rejected by CRA et al, after reviewing documentary evidence and probable cause analyses augmented by a National Weather Service (NOAA) reevaluation of November 10th storm conditions; a degraded maintenance and repair condition of the vessel; and the abnormal hydrostatic and hydrodynamic Constructive Interference Wave (or Rogue Wave-Wall of Water) effects.

Under these surface breakup conditions, the potential terminal destructive effects of grounding on a shoal(s) or impacting a submerged shipwreck(s) would have been nullified.

- 14.0 -
STORM EFFECTS

Re: Seiche-Surge-Clapotis Fitzgerald Meets The Witch Of November

The most probable tracks and positions of the Edmund Fitzgerald and Arthur M. Anderson based upon reports of their position and information were contained in the NTSB Report and the final position of the Edmund Fitzgerald is 46° 59.9′ N, 85° 06.6′ W, about 17 miles from the entrance to Whitefish Bay, Michigan.

The November 10th 1975 Lake Superior wave system had individual and collective destructive energy generated by a confluence of *seiche, surge and clapotic* (Constructive Interference) wave action, that would have overtaken the relatively-slower Fitzgerald from almost full-astern, as determined by the Author.

Such a Constructive Interference Wave system has capability to momentarily <u>double</u> prevailing significant wave heights (to about 80 feet) with devastating hydrostatic and hydrodynamic force effects on a stern-

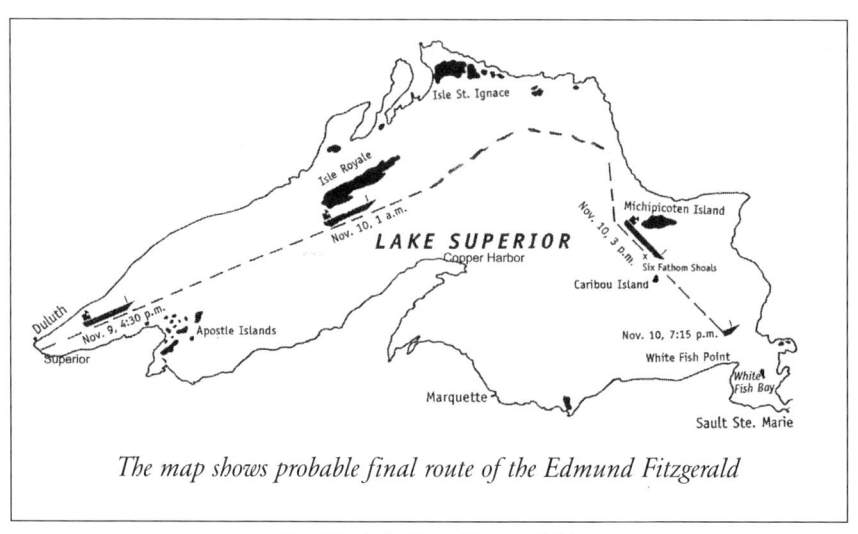

The map shows probable final route of the Edmund Fitzgerald

Z= "Zulu" time (Greenwich)

plunging Fitzgerald. The seiche component could have also cyclically acted to reduce water depth over shoaling areas.

Voyage reconstruction confirmed that the Fitzgerald was "pooped", by enormous wave troughs and crests collectively passing <u>under and over the stern and across the starboard stern quarter</u>...as similarly experienced by the Anderson during Captain Cooper's reported (lesser extent) encounter with an abnormal "3-Sisters" boarding wave system.

A combination of "over-the-starboard-quarter" astern pooping and downward (stern) plunging action, under multi-directional hydrostatic and hydrodynamic forces would have buckled and breached the aftermost (No. 21) hatch cover and others immediately forward of the poop deckhouse front-and now hidden below the inverted stern section.

With higher-speed overtaking seas engulfing the starboard stern and causing asymmetric loading of the hull structure, an induced starboard roll could have degenerated to a permanent listing condition, when progressive cargo hatch cover breaching would have led to uncontrolled rapid flooding of No. 7 water ballast tank (starboard) and No. 3 Cargo Hold.

Concurrently, asymmetric loading forces would have induced torsional hull stressing which, in combination with the hull structural fracture and stern separation at about Frame 178, would have made major contribution to the sinking casualty and rotational stern breakaway.

The Lake Superior storm dynamics of November 10th 1975, that were recently reanalyzed in May 2006 by Hurltquist NOAA (NWS), provided reasonable verification of the CRA literature search discoveries.

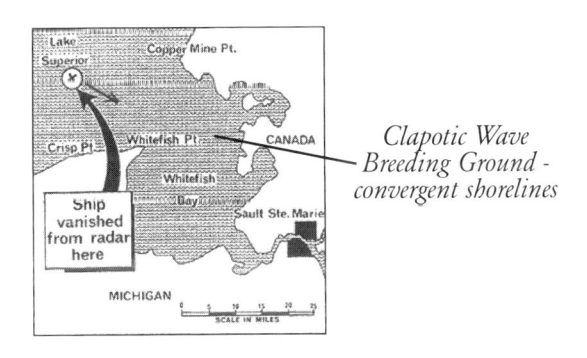

Clapotic Wave Breeding Ground - convergent shorelines

FITZGERALD MEETS THE WITCH OF NOVEMBER

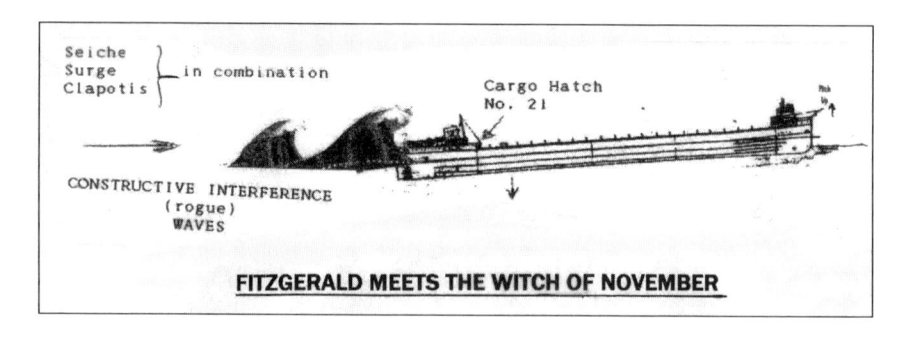

Unusual shore-reflected (clapotic) waves were recorded by NOAA when acting perpendicular to the vessel's track toward Whitefish Bay, Michigan as stated in the Author's reconstruction of the storm and ship tracking scenario. Compensatory vessel heading correction and speed reduction would have been necessary to change the frequency and severity of bow wave encounter.

The latter waves became unified in confluence with a down-bound lethal *Constructive Interference Wave* system, that gained incredible strength through augmentation with *seiche, surge and clapotic* destructive wave forces that caused irreversible hull fracture in a matter of seconds.

A rudimentary description for such a lethal wave condition, inclusive of the fatal over-the-stern "pooping" of S.S. Edmund Fitzgerald, (with approximate scaling), is illustrated on following pages.

Anatomy And Effects Of A Lethal Constructive Interference (Rogue) Wave Condition. (Freak) (Episodic) (Wall Of Water) (Hole in The Sea) at Whitefish Bay, Michigan on November 10th 1975.

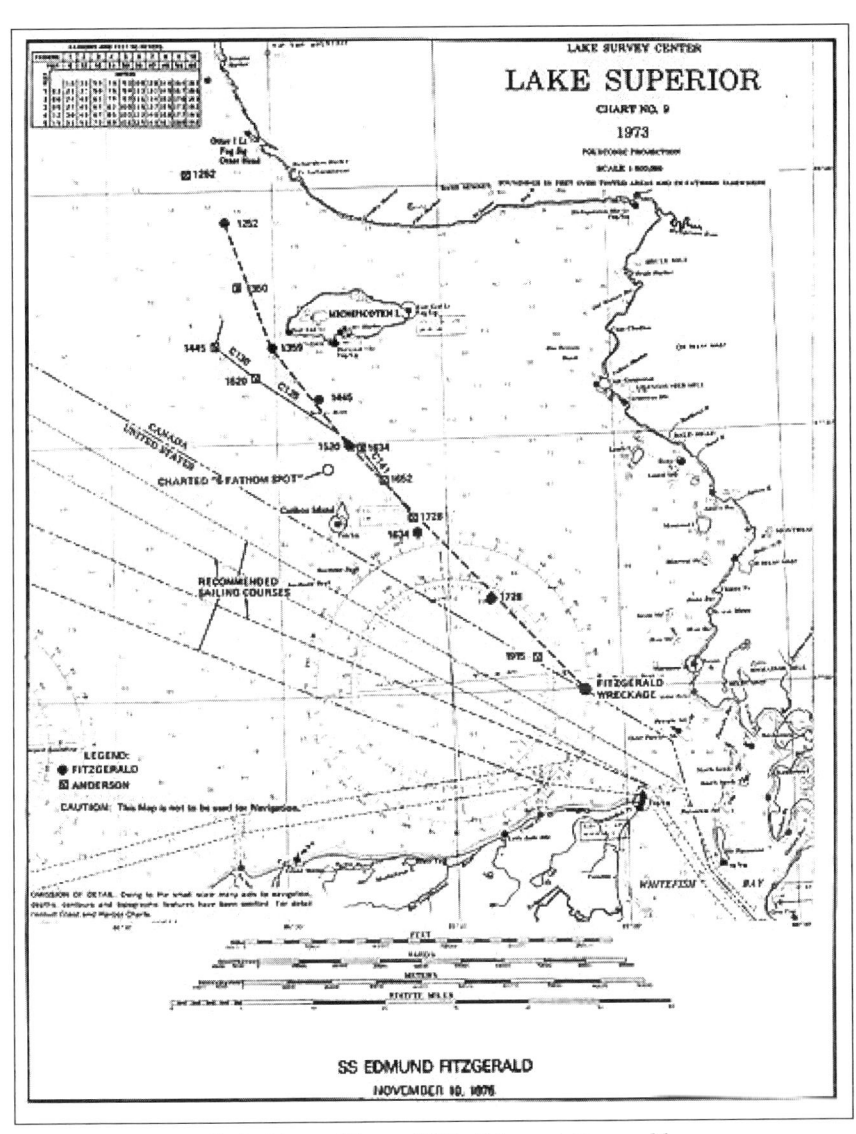

*Probable tracklines of S.S. Edmund Fitzgerald
and S.S. Arthur M. Anderson on Novemeber 10, 1975.*

A more comprehensive understanding of hull structural behavior, destructive storm wave and weather patterning, and ship response dynamics is available through companion book "For Whom The Bells Toll" which was published in 2006 by the Dorance Publishing Company, Pittsburgh.

Situation

During Fitzgerald's final approach to Whitefish Bay, it was determined that the vessel was transitting under rapidly deteriorating storm conditions, with near hurricane-force northwest winds and abnormal wave heights. A storm reanalysis was recently made by The National Weather Service (in May 2006) (by Hurltquist et al) for storm development and hindsight estimation showing that any ship following a similar course to Fitzgerald, but six hours earlier or later, would have avoided the worst storm conditions.

Seiche

This environmental condition was generated in concert with a high-pressure region over Duluth and Thunder Bay regions. The increasing northwest winds propelled large masses of water toward a very low-pressure atmospheric condition positioned over Marquette...and created a powerful <u>Seiche</u> with a <u>sloshing back and forth effect</u> in the enclosed "bath-tub" containment.

This natural phenomena also caused alternating increases and decreases of the water levels at opposite ends of Lake Superior, with resultant overriding of closed SOO Lock gates.

Surging

Additive wave force and motion (<u>without a sloshing back and forth effect</u>) could have been unidirectionally headed toward Whitefish Bay, driven by the extremely high winds from the Northwest.

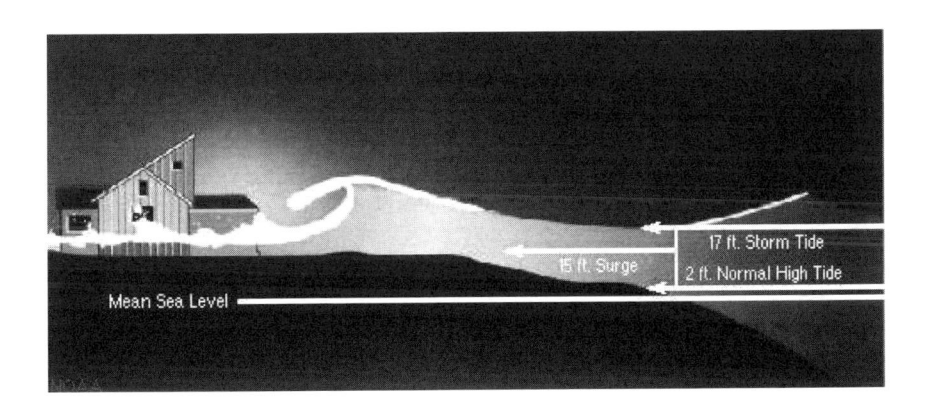

[Figure: Storm surge diagram showing Mean Sea Level, 15 ft. Surge, 2 ft. Normal High Tide, and 17 ft. Storm Tide]

Storm Surge

The low-lying areas were particularly vulnerable to the wall of water that storms sent ashore.

Clapotis

These are "<u>clapping</u>" waves which would have been generated by the reflection of down-bound waves off steep, cliff-like and convergent USA/Canada underwater coastlines...and a credible cause of wave energy reversal.

Such wave response was recorded <u>perpendicular</u> to Fitzgerald's down-bound track, and contributory to a three-hundred (300) mile down-bound fetch, combining sciche, surge and other destructive wind and wave-generated influences.

In full <u>clapotis</u>, both crests and troughs had capability to d<u>ouble</u> the height of normal waves, while <u>twice</u> in each wave period the water surface would be momentarily <u>flat</u>.

Bottom Topography And Water Depth.

Shallowing water and underwater formations would have also added <u>ac</u>celerative wave energy to the foregoing destructive forces...which would have had storm-driven wind and wave confluence near the <u>wedge-shaped</u> Whitefish Bay entrance.

This generally explains the abnormally steep and dangerous wave confluence that could have been encountered by the Fitzgerald in her final approach to Whitefish Bay under shallowing water conditions.

In rationalizing why <u>Anderson</u> survived and <u>Fitzgerald</u> did not, it appears credible that:

- The Anderson, was a stiffer hull and was about ten (10) miles astern. She also was more distant from convergent and reflective shoreline boundaries, which were at a different, less-destructive locations relative to the <u>Constructive Interference Wave</u> epicenter.
- The <u>thirty-five</u> (35) foot waves experienced by the S.S. Arthur M. Anderson, may have been of lesser height and energy...and not the higher "<u>Walls of Water</u>" as encountered by Fitzgerald and up-bound "saltie" M.V. Avafors.
- The described confluence would have uniquely placed the Fitzgerald at "the wrong place at the wrong time," in a lethal <u>Constructive Interference Wave</u>-generating environment...which was conducive to combining the destructive forces of considerably magnified wave formations.

For a more comprehensive appreciation of this natural phenomena I recommend viewing History Channel DVD. CAT NO. AAE 76081 RE: "Rogue Waves." a 50-minute documentary.

- 15.0 -
CIRCUMSTANTIAL PROPOSITIONS

The following propositions are believed to be worthy of inclusion in the extant repertoire of others seeking to unravel the Fitzgerald catastrophe:

Lemma 1

The *Fitzgerald's* pre-sinking operating circumstances may be realistically represented by hull casualty impairment, dependency on remote navigational guidance, deferred hull repair and maintenance and the encountering of environmental chaos having abnormal natural forces seeking out the "Achilles Heel" of her marine system.

Lemma 2

The fatal scenario clearly portrays the listing vessel, with lost buoyancy due to initial bow-damage and one breached side tunnel, in a condition of operational extremus while underway. She was subjected to a violent northwest (135° T) Lake Superior storm, which overtook the vessel from almost full-astern when on down-bound course 141° T en-route to Whitefish Bay. In nautical terms, the vessel would most certainly have been "pooped" by waves of enormous height, mass and energy, with troughs and crests collectively passing under and over her stern and across the starboard stern quarter superstructure. Additionally the vessel would have subsequently experienced the devastating effects of "Constructive Interference Waves" when entering a convergent land-mass zone conducive to the generation of clapotic waves and possibly the powerful Lake Superior seiche and storm surge effects driven by the storm.

Lemma 3

The vessel was capably manned and held necessary seaworthiness certifications after recently passing USCG/ABS inspections, and she was under command of an experienced master, with qualified officers and crew members aboard. <u>No fatal shoaling damage is believed to have been sustained during transit.</u>

Lemma 4

It is highly probable that the wheelsman was able to compensate for any heading control difficulties caused by asymmetric buoyancy losses in the bow compartments and the added weight of the water flooding the tunnel compartment on one side of the vessel following *U.F.O. impact. Underwater surveys of the inverted stern indicated <u>an offset rudder angle of up to ten degrees, possible reflecting the wheelsman's compensatory action to maintain a favorable heading.</u>

Footnote: Lemmas are propositions proved, or sometimes assumed to be true and used in proving a theorum. (Webster)
*UFO Unidentified Floating Object

Lemma 5

The vessel was experiencing extraordinary November storm conditions from the northwest when steaming toward the eastern terminus of Lake Superior and within seventeen miles of safe haven at Whitefish Bay, Michigan.

The rapidly converging American/Canadian shorelines, with steep underwater cliff frontage, were capable of reflecting incoming trans-lake waves. Ensuing wave generation could be expected to augment downbound, storm-driven trans-lake waves to form destructive and episodic "wall of water" conditions having abnormal height and energy. When combined with "pooping" waves and plunging of the stern, the vessel's stern would have become overwhelmed and certain cargo hatch covers immediately forward of the poop front would have been breached...prior to rapid flooding.

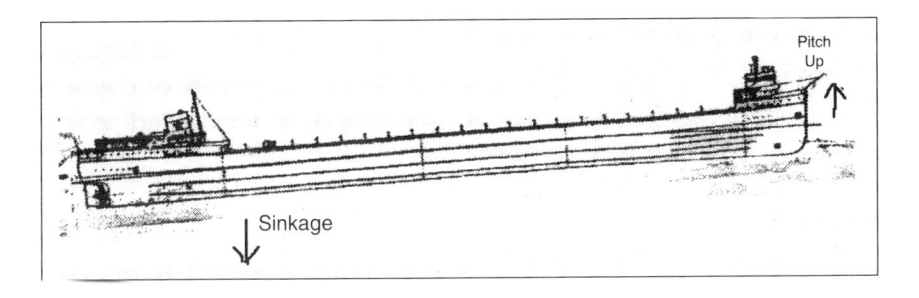

Lemma 6

Wave troughs advancing below the stern and (seventy-foot) "Constructive Wave" crests periodically overtaking ("pooping") the vessel's starboard stern quarter would have induced significant stern sinkage and listing when experiencing dynamic plunging motions. Coupled with rapid water ingress through the aftermost breached cargo hatches, a permanent increase in stern immersion would have made the vessel "stern heavy." Progressively increasing water inundation of cargo holds would have immediately followed as the vessel began to list and sink *stern first*.

Estimated time to fill (159, 510 Cub. Ft.) *void space above* taconite in No. 3 Cargo Hold (only) subsequent to breaching of hatch cover(s):

Waterhead Height and Inflow Rate	Hatch Covers Breached (No. 3 Cargo Hold Only)		
	21	21 and 20	21, 20 and 19
	Fill Time (secs)	Fill Time (secs)	Fill Time (secs)
20 ft. waterhead @ 316 tons/sec	14.0	7.0	4.7
40 ft. waterhead @ 446 tons/sec	9.9	5.0	3.3
70 ft. waterhead @ 591 tons/sec	7.5	3.8	2.5

N.B. - Rapid vessel sinkage assumed to preempt consideration of lake water appreciably permeating the interstices of stowed taconite pellet cargo.

Lemma 7

The vessel could have been expected to retain a reducing amount of residual forward momentum with multiple degrees of dynamic motion, as the vessel rapidly lost reserve buoyancy in a severely stern-trimmed condition that progressively added lake water weight (est. 12,300 tons) in the void space above the stowed taconite ore in *all* cargo holds. Taconite ore shifting in a sternward direction within No. 3 Cargo Hold would have contributed to the vessel's increasing stern sinkage demise.

Upon flooding of the machinery space and cessation of propulsion power, the vessel's residual momentum would have continued to facilitate forward motion for a very limited distance (est. one-half mile/four ship lengths), before progressive filling of No. 1 and No. 2 Cargo Holds and simultaneous submergence.

Lemma 8

While on the surface in an unrecoverable stern-heavy condition, and with pitching downward motion of the bow, the *Fitzgerald's* hall girder would have experienced non-uniform distributive loading conditions as the after end of the vessel increased in weight due to flooding, dynamic boarding seas, and the sternward shifting of cargo. The dynamic motions of the vessel, and superimposed external loading, would have induced excessive hogging (bending upward), causing failure of the longitudinal hull girder as the bending, shearing and torsional strength capabilities were exceeded.

At this juncture a propagative spar deck rupture condition at frame 178 (but not total hull separation) would have developed at about the mid-length of No. 3 Cargo Hold, as recorded on videotape, and immediately prior to stern breakaway and the onset of rapid hull submergence.

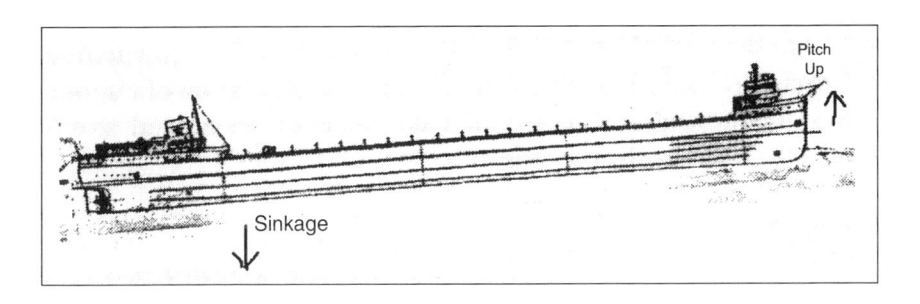

In the process:
- The shell and cargo hold plating, boundaries of Starboard Ballast Tank No. 7 would have also been fractured thereby causing localized flooding with a further loss in reserve buoyancy;
- Lake water entrapped in the tunnel would have also been released; and
- Uncontrolled flooding of No. 3 Cargo Hold, with taconite ore spillage and shifting, would have commenced.

Lemma 9

On each side of the hull rupture, taconite would have been spilled, causing shifts in the longitudinal centers of gravity of the conjoined 240-foot stern and 489-foot bow section that was submerging with a slowing, forward bow-down trajectory.

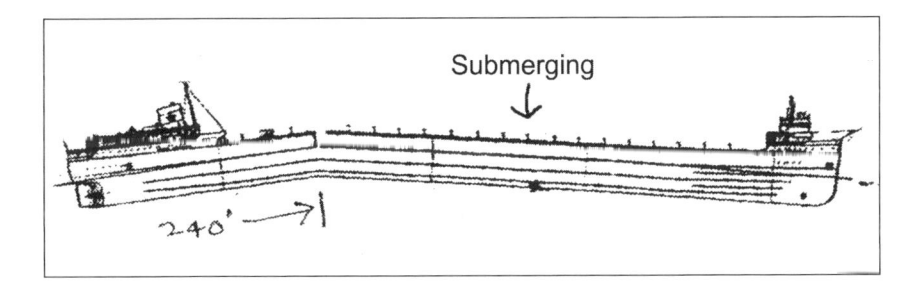

Lemma 10

It is considered likely that the hinged downward 240-foot stern section could have become separated and capsized during submergence within the water column as it became fully rotated to a final inverted position *before* the inclined bow plowed into the lake floor to a penetration depth of about twenty-seven feet, and with an inclination of about fifteen degrees. It is also possible that the stern section descent was at a *lesser* rate than the taconite-laden 489-foot bow section, because of hydrodynamic resistance (bluntness) at the stern hull separation facing forward.

A 213-foot cargo hold section appears to have separated *after* the 489-foot bow section forcefully penetrated the lake floor to a depth of about twenty-seven feet, with an inclination of about fifteen degrees.

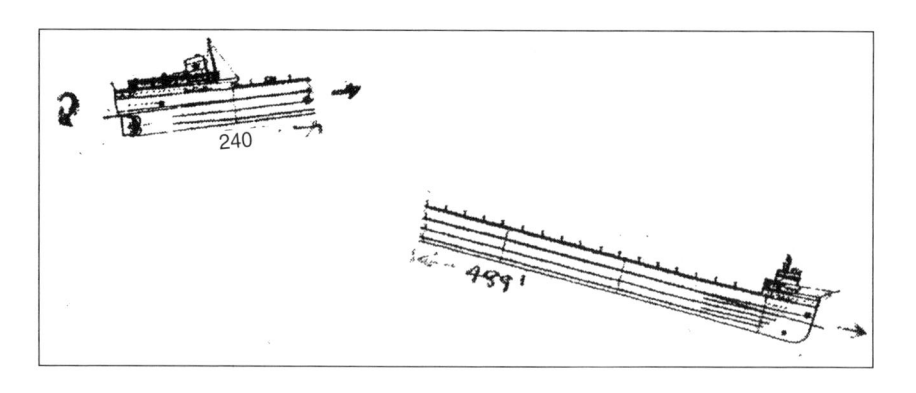

In this position, the bow was placed in a cantilevered loading condition vulnerable to separation into a forward 276-foot length and a dislocated 213-foot center section due to cargo shifting and bottom impact. This 213-foot section was later identified as "An area of distorted metal lying between the two (separated bow and stern) sections, and to both sides over a distance of some 200 feet." Part of the devastated 213-foot center cargo hold section does rest between the sunken bow and stern, and a portion could be entrapped below the inverted stern.

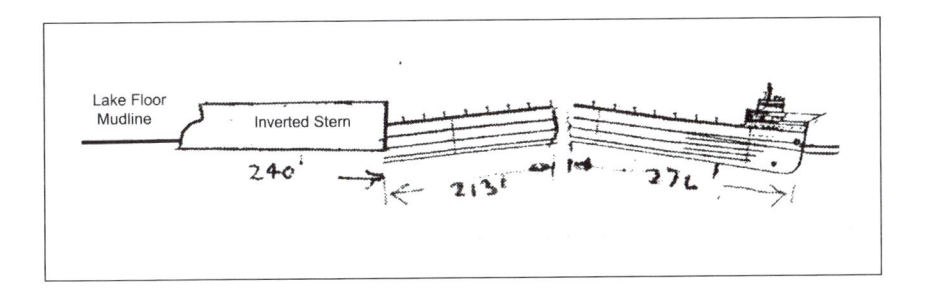

After the sinking, steel cargo-hold hatch covers and coamings were observed to be in many forms of implosion, explosion, dislodgement, and release, which may be attributable to external hydrostatic pressure instability (buckling) failures and internal air or explosion pressurization causing release.

Lemma 11

With the increasing depth of submergence, hydrostatic pressure equalization should have progressively collapsed the boundaries of side ballast and other tankage (during pressure equalization), as recorded by videotape. A domino-effect of co-dependent structural failures would also be present during submergence to a maximum depth of 530 feet (230 psi).

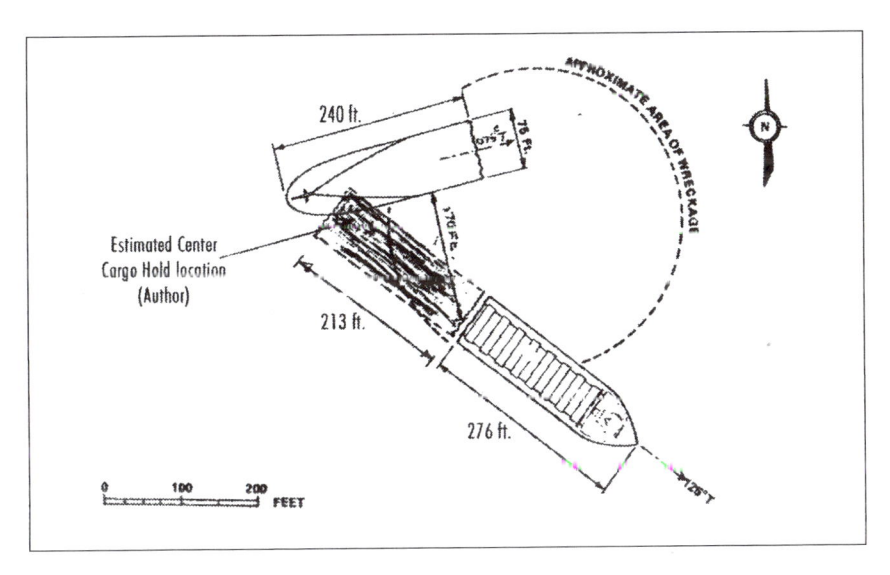

Lemma 12

If the structural and watertight integrity of the *Fitzgerald's* hull envelope and cargo hatches had remained intact, her stern should have subsequently risen in response to the dynamic redistribution of overall hull buoyancy and the attendant center of buoyancy adjustments.

Should such favorable circumstances have prevailed, the author considers that, with adequate reserve buoyancy from her (empty) ballast tankage, survivability would have been viable over the final seventeen-mile transit.

Note: It was reported that it would require flooding of <u>more than three adjacent ballast tanks, on the same side</u> of the vessel, for capsizing to occur.

Lemma 13

Crew members were unable to escape or survive due to:
- The vessel's catastrophic and rapid sinking mode;
- The inability to gain access to, or launch, lifeboats or life-rafts when overtaken by boarding seas having abnormal "Constructive Interference Waves";
- The absence of an autonomous-ejectable survival module(s), which was neither specified nor available; and
- Lack of exposure suit equipment, which was neither specified nor available.

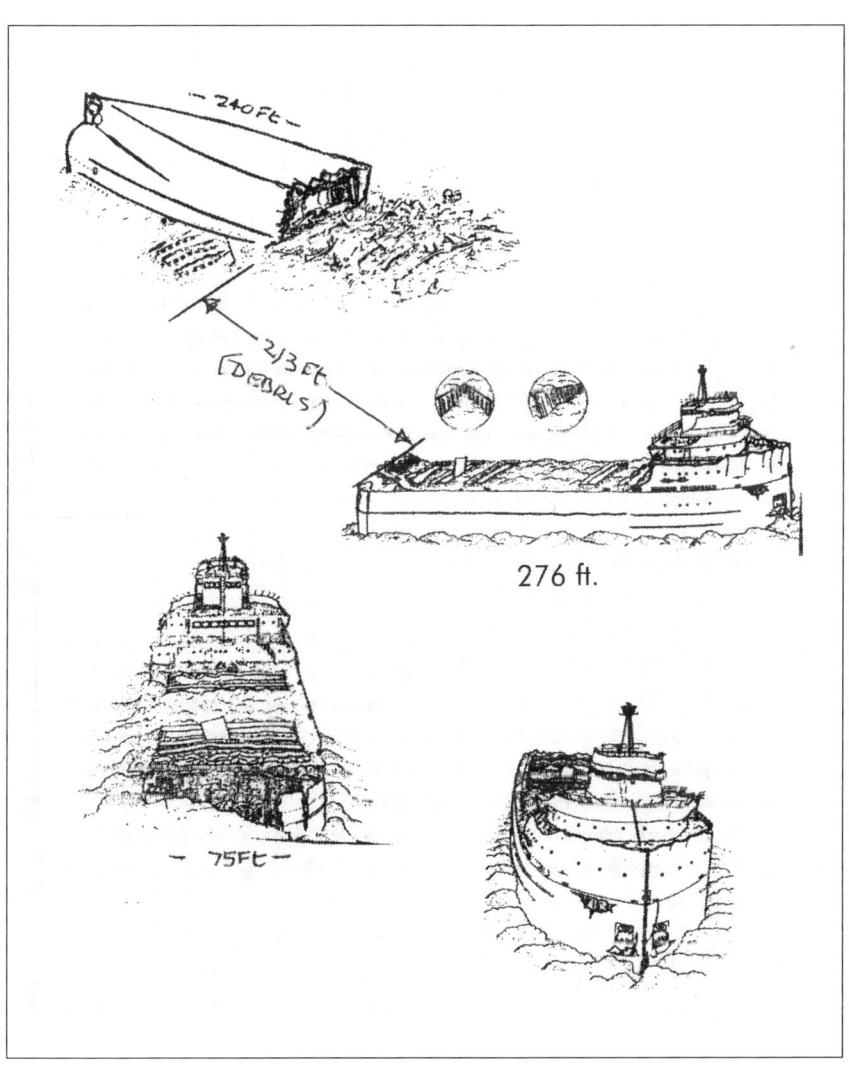

Image Courtesy of U.S.C.G.

- 16.0 -
CARGO HOLD FLOODING

Since high-density iron-ore cargo occupies about 50% of a cargo hold's (volumetric) capacity, the upper 50% is void with an un-impeded flooding rate, subsequent to hatch cover buckling and breaching.

Lake water inundation through only *one* (11'0" x 48'0") cargo hatch opening, with a dynamic water-head of only *twenty-feet*, was estimated to take about *fourteen* (14) seconds...and this should enable understanding of Fitzgerald's rapid disappearance without survivors.

For reader perspective, the following provides order of magnitude estimations of water ingress through each breached 48-foot x 11-foot cargo hatch opening, when exposed to various steady state water-head heights:

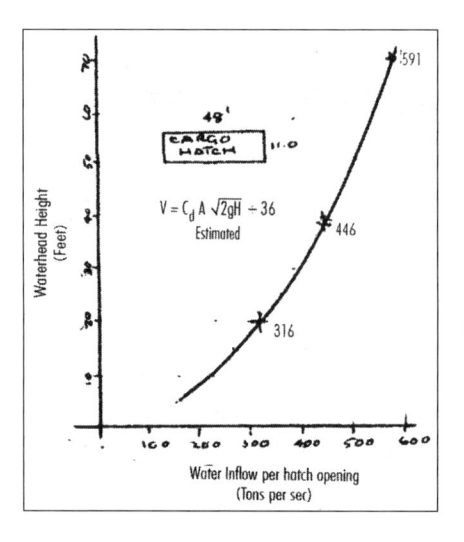

Order of Magnitude Time Lapse Estimation for
Flooding Void Cargo Hold Volume
(above Taconite)

Cargo hold gross volume 860,950 cub. ft.
Cargo hold total length 519 feet.
Cargo weight 26,1161 L. Tons
Cargo volume 417,856 Cub. Ft.

$V = C_d A \sqrt{2gH} \div 36$ Estimated

Cargo Hold	No. 1	No. 2	No. 3
Length in feet.	177	144	198
Gross Hold Volume (Cub. Ft.)	309,942	241,066	309,942
	(36%)	(28%)	(36%)
Ore Cargo Weight (Long Tons)	9,402	7,312	9,402
Ore Volume (@ 16 Cub. Ft/Ton)	150,432	116,991	150,432
Void Hold Volume (Cub. Ft.) Above Ore Cargo	159,510	124,075	159,510
*Flooding Capacity (Long Tons) (If void hold volume filled with water @ 36 Cub. Ft./Ton)	4,431	3,447	4,431

Estimated Time to Fill <u>No. 3 Cargo Hold Void Space</u> (After Breaching of After Hatch Covers Nos. 21 or 21, 20 or 21, 20,19).

Waterhead Height and Inflow Rate	Hatch Covers Breached (No. 3 Cargo Hold Only)		
	21	21 and 20	21, 20 and 19
	Fill Time (secs)	Fill Time (secs)	Fill Time (secs)
20 ft. waterhead @ 316 tons/sec	14.0	7.0	4.7
40 ft. waterhead @ 446 tons/sec	9.9	5.0	3.3
70 ft. waterhead @ 591 tons/sec	7.5	3.8	2.5

* No allowance was made for cargo permeability since the time lapse for flooding and taconite penetration was minimal.

To fully appreciate the destructive natural synergy that enveloped *Fitzgerald*, one is required to juxtapose dynamic vessel motions upon the overwhelming storm wave formations advancing from astern with a speed of advance greater than that of the vessel itself. For purposes of this brief treatise, the confluence of forces could include, but not be restricted to observations of Captain Cooper *et al*:

Storm Speed of Advance . . . . 40mph. . . . (Est)
Vessel Speed of Advance. . . . . 16.3 mph . . . (max)
Vessel Course (Down-bound) . . . . 141° T
Storm Vector (from Astern) . . . . 135° T
Wind Speed . . . . 80 mph   (min)
Wave Crest Spacing . . . . 250 ft. . . . (Est)
Trans-Lake ("pooping") Wave heights* . . . . . . 40 ft. . . . (min)
"Constructive Interference Wave" Heights . . . 70 ft. . . . . (Est)

- 17.0 -
EPILOGUE

The following closing comments are mainly relative to the Author's professional concerns about a continuing hiatus in providing technical and legal closure to the inconclusive public hearings on the S.S. Edmund Fitzgerald sinking loss of November 10th 1975.

And, Casualty Research Associates (CRA) wishes to make it known that, during an initial high-level Washington informational exchange in advance preparation for the book "For Whom The Bells Toll," the Author was unexpectedly taken aback when cautioned (and became initially aware of) a biased and inflammatory organizational position entrenched in such statements as "Captain McSorley killed those guys!" and "Be careful what you say and write around here because this place is "crawling" with a lot of "Coasties" (ex-United State Coast Guard) retirees!"

As a Washingtonian for over forty years, I was already well apprised of employment "revolving doors" that facilitate high-level transitions from uniformed cultures to U.S. Civil Service (double-dipping) and private sector employment, positions..._without_ regard to carryover conflicts of interest between ex-regulators and those they previously regulated.

The Author was undeterred and found such "enlightenment" to be only partially true and mentally filed away this negativity, as Findings of Fact and truth were pursued on a <u>voluntary</u> basis for book preparation. In collaboration with Casualty Research Associates (CRA), end goals were planned to include the challenging obfuscation, "zippered lips," and brain-teasing conjecture surrounding "Fitzgerald's" mystery and mystique.

Part of the CRA strategy is to seek truth and voluntarily promote a humanitarian basis for harmed "Fitzgerald" family member survivors to achieve psychological closure and to justify more appropriate compensation via a public rehearing, under the *unbiased* aegis of the U.S. Judiciary (versus the regulatory United States Coast Guard-USCG) organization. Press releases of the 1970's closely monitored the limited public hearing process when:

> Mr. John J. Dwyer, president of Oglebay Norton (Fitzgerald charterer) said, "In the interest of all who sail the Great Lakes, we must do everything possible to determine the cause of the sinking of Fitzgerald."

"Oglebay Norton is in close touch with every family to make sure that none lacks the *immediate* financial support it needs" he added. However, it is known that some of the mariners died intestate and were required to settle claims pursuant to time-consuming Probate Court procedures which incurred significant delays and hardship.

> The aggrieved family survivors expeditiously received modest monetary amounts determined by the Oglebay Norton Company of 1210 Hanna Building, Cleveland Ohio 44115, a corporation, and the S.S. Edmund Fitzgerald bare-boat charterer, from the shipowner Northwestern Mutual Life Insurance Company of 720 East Wisconsin Avenue, Milwaukee, Wisconsin 53202.

Compensatory payments were made promptly by Oglebay Norton in amounts determined by *that* Company, and nominally about twelve months *in advance* of accident official findings reported on (May 04 1978) by the National Transportation Safety Board (NTSB), subsequent to adjournment of public hearings conducted by the United States Coast Guard Marine Board of Investigation.

> (1) *The Oglebay Norton Company determination of specific monetary amounts and the payment scheduling thereof with binding (gag-order) payee conditions, were considered to be prematurely untimely prior to the official release of probable cause(s) for the final ship casualty and Board determination(s) of organizational culpability.*

An in-hand Receipt and Release legal agreement reveals that payer parties (Oglebay Norton Company et al) were absolved from any and all payee claim, action, cause, demands of every cause or nature, for compensation pursuant to vulnerable-survivor acceptance of this mutual agreement...and with pre-emption of awaited official Board outcomes.

> (2) Board of Inquiry chairman Rear Adm. Winford H. Barrow USCG, said (When the hearings adjourned) "The testimony indicated it (the ship) broke up rather suddenly, catastrophically."

No specifics were given to account for why, or which parties were responsible. This bland statement was considered to be premature and untimely due the potential influence of structural design inadequacies, maintenance and repair negligence as probable causes(s) for the ship casualty and Board determination(s) of organizational culpability.

The National Transportation Safety Board (NTSB) exercised their primacy authority and made recommendations independently. They were not in full agreement with those reported by the USCG Marine Board of Investigation Report No. 16732/64216 which provided indefinite rationale and an inadequate statement that "*The proximate cause for loss of the S.S. Edmund Fitzgerald cannot be determined.* i.e. They failed to meet the lawful requirements of Section 6301 of Title 46, United States Code, and USCG Regulation 46 CFR Part 4 having stipulation that:

> (i) The USCG conduct a marine casualty investigation to determine the cause of the casualty. (which was not achieved)
> (ii) The cause of any (of the 29 deaths, (which was not achieved). and without stating:
> (iii) Whether the casualty should be further investigated by a Marine Board of Investigation, in accordance with USCG Regulation 46 CFR 4.09/4.07-1
> (iv) Other related investigative factors were not identified.

The public hearing brevity, with inconclusive and controversial reported findings, failed to provide comprehensive points of reference as necessary:

> (a) For Mr. Dwyer to identify well-intentional "appropriate" levels of surviving family compensation, in advance of Marine Board determinations findings and recommendations was considered premature and presumptive, due to a then-<u>unstated</u> (*shipowner*) burden of liability, having legal premising on:
>> *"If vessel is lost due to shipowner (Northwestern Mutual Life Insurance Company) negligence to keep and maintain a safe vessel, then that shipowner is financially liable for most of the loss suffered."*
>
> (b) Admiral Barrow's premature postulation of the casualty failure mode, in advance of official NTSB and USCG Marine Board releases with respect to determinations, findings and recommendations for the Fitzgerald sinking based on the paucity and inconclusive nature of technical testimony, is considered to be in non-compliance with Title 46 USC and USCG CFR requirements.

The absence of crew survivor witnesses, and without full technical knowledge of deferred structurally-critical ship maintenance, repair and neglected hull reinforcement commensurate with deeper-draft operation. Increased cargo hauling capability (coupled with the questionable accuracy of in-transit testimony), required finalized Board decisional analysis and resolution *before* any official public statements or claimant actions should be initiated.

In contrast, the S.S. Carl D. Bradley's final public hearing report was promulgated on July 7th 1959 about <u>eight</u> (8) months <u>after</u> the November 18th 1958 sinking.

The Fitzgerald's Board's expost facto failure to achieve unanimity and formation of acceptable decisional parameters is still (generally) considered to have placed impediments in probable-cause pathways to meaningful case resolution for Fitzgerald under prevailing (1975) circumstances. There appears to be justifiable cause for conduct of a *District*

Court rehearing, even though an appointed Marine Casualty Investigating Board Chairman represents the Department of Justice per P.L. 74-622 (1936).

To date, CRA has solicited surviving family interest in the formation of a (rehearing) constituency named Great Lakes Family Association (GLFA) patterned after the self-managed British M.V. Derbyshire (Oil/Bulk/Ore) carrier Families Association (DFA) that successfully established political and monetary support from Members of Parliament legislators for investigation and rehearing in their High Court of Justice (Admiralty) regarding the vessel's unexplained sinking, with justification based on biased procrastinating by lower-level, non-judicial hearing panelist deliberations.

Response from Fitzgerald's survivor families has not been overwhelming, since most families claim that they are bound by an employee/employer agreement to cease and desist in any spoken or written communication regarding the Fitzgerald operation or sinking. (i.e. A perceived "gag order" which will require removal to facilitate testimony and CRA discussion). Otherwise, an expression of non-interest from survivor families of Fitzgerald and other Lakers should be honored.

Under the Fitzgerald's sinking circumstances during severe November storm conditions on Lake Superior (in an authorized overloaded condition *without* additional hull structural reinforcement and without adequate life-cycle maintenance and repairs), CRA considers that the preponderance of evidence justifies official exoneration of the vessel's master Captain Ernest M. McSorley, his officers and crew members...

May they all rest in peace, since sinking causes and effects, now known to CRA, are supported by evidentiary proof and are consistent with NTSB Findings of Fact and CRA taped and photographic discoveries, which provide confirmation that navigational errors *did not* contribute to catastrophic hull damage caused by shoaling; or that incipient hatch cover gasket leakage could have caused significant reserve buoyancy loss due to crew negligence in the securing of Kestner clamps to maintain hatch cover weather-tightness during abnormal boarding sea conditions.

CRA et al concur with NTSB findings and conclusions that <u>catastrophic</u> massive cargo hold flooding was <u>due to hatch cover collapse</u> (implosion under storm conditions). This finding has no relationship with alleged <u>incipient</u> hatch cover perimeter gasket leakage supposedly attributable to crew negligence.

This is verifiable by post-hearing technical evidence discoveries confirming regulatory negligence, confiscation of maintenance records, and by failing to design and incorporate additional hull envelope and hatch cover reinforcement to ensure ship reserve buoyancy integrity...commensurate with the reduced Winter freeboard (increased draft of 3' 3/1/4") authorized by Great Lakes Load Line Regulation amendment 46 CFR 45.5

This amendment corresponded to about a 4,000 ton structural overload in cargo deadweight capacity causing hull stress elevation and increased flexure; and almost a doubling of static water pressure from boarding sea loading on submerged cargo hatch covers and coamings <u>(which failed under subsequent NTSB testing)</u>.

Verifiable hull structural weaknesses are traceable to extrapolated design practices *without* supportive Research, Development, Test and Evaluation (RDT&E), coupled with questionable production and fabricated material quality controls (which were <u>outside</u> operating mariner purview).

Verifiable evidentiary discoveries of vessel maintenance and repair negligence are detrimental to mariner safety and seaworthiness, in the legal custody of the Fitzgerald charterer as the shipowners surrogate.

The Author, as possibly the last remaining member of Great Lakes Engineering Works hull design staff who technically supported the S.S. Fitzgerald (Hull 301), has herewith objectively provided information usually reserved for company "insiders" who were generally bound by traditional Great lakes shipbuilding practices and customs. Denial of the Author's pre delivery (1958) requests to develop naval architectural cargo and ballasting loading manuals, inclining experiment (stability) procedures, and outfitting allowance for a fathometer and an Emergency Positioning Indication Beacon (EPIRB), typify deficient regulatory safety situation(s) needed to be made known for The Record.

In some instances the root causes of these omissions are traceable to (1950's) technical specification shortfalls of USCG Load Line Regulations.

In closing I would like to cite a choice Americanism, by stating that it is too late to put Fitzgerald's hull structural "*toothpaste*" and maintenance neglect back into its tube...except for supporting the surviving family rehearing.

Although CRA's technical and operational research has (now) enabled better understanding of Fitzgerald's design, construction and working environment, it has unexpectedly exposed the personal financial concerns of surviving mariner families, in addition to the vessel's overloaded and deteriorated structural conditions which were exacerbated by driven-hard life-cycle that should *never again be replicated.*

- 17.1 -
TOWARD JUSTICE AND KINDER TIMES

The author's review of reported approaches to liability claim(s) resolution for deceased crew victims of the S.S. Edmund Fitzgerald (November 10th 1975) and the S.S. Carl D. Bradley (November 18 1958) sinkings, revealed that the latter vessel was older and originally built in 1927 for the Bradley Transportation Company of Rogers City, Michigan, and victim lawsuits were filed for more than sixteen (16) million dollars. On December 5th 1959, settlement was made whereby the final ship-owner (United States Steel Corporation) set aside $1,250,000 for all claims.

Recommendations for sharing of the settlement fund, for the latter vessel, were filed in U.S. District Court on June 13th 1960 did (correctly) antedate public hearing outcomes reported to the USCG Commandment on July 7th 1959.

Judge Charles J. McNamee appointed Cleveland lawyer Jerome N. Curtis Esq. as commissioner to take testimony on the claims and to recommend Bradley survivor family apportionments (Appendix II), which eventually considered average earnings, length of service, life expectancy and family status. Attorney Curtis held hearings in Rogers City, Detroit and Cleveland.

To date, the author has been unable to identify similar (proper) legal procedural actions for the S.S. Edmund Fitzgerald, for other than suits filed by two crew plaintiffs against (ship owner) <u>Northwestern Mutual Life Insurance Company</u> on November 17th 1975...prior to the promulgation of primacy Report NTSB MAR-78-3 determinations and findings and recommendations of May 4 1978.

With acknowledgment of apparent public hearing irregularities and inconclusive outcomes of the abbreviated public hearing process, the Author and Associates have found a dearth and withholding of information regarding victim family participation in the monetary compensation rationale for each payment determination made by the Oglebay Norton

Company vessel *charterer* (emphasis added).

It is preferred that the legal administration and District Court filings related to compensatory payments should have been made by the *shipowner* and not the charterer, with respect to venue, scheduling, and monetary amounts. Both actions were considered technically and administratively premature and were never challenged or accepted by Fitzgerald's families with legal counsel assistance, since:

> (1) The NTSB primacy Report Mar-78-3 of May 4th 1978 determinations and findings had *not* been promulgated for public use.
> (2) Apart from (premature) lawsuits which were independently filed in District Court by the legal counsel for two Fitzgerald mariner families, *no* evidence came to light designating a court-appointed commissioner having a responsibility assignment to:
>> - Document survivor family testimony on each claim, and to
>> - Recommend apportionments which would consider average earnings, length of service, life expectancy and family status (per the Bradley model).

From the Fitzgerald surviving family point of view it would appear that other steps toward personal closure would be to seek as minimum, an appointment of a *U.S. District Court* commissioner, to:

> - Petition Congressional representatives for Fitzgerald rehearings to be conducted in U.S. District Court. (a-1a M.V.Derbyshire strategy)
> - Annulment of any and all surviving family loss-compensation "gag orders" on Fitzgerald information exchanges.
> - Petition for the *shipowner* Northwestern Mutual Life Insurance Company (versus Oglebay Norton-vessel charterer) to be recognized as the culpable Defendant.
> - Review and amend *premature* Oglebay Norton survivor payment rationale and disbursement procedures that preceded determination of official identification of the ship casualty *probable causes*, and Board inconclusive prognostications of organizational *culpability*.

To seek justice *independently* from numerous overwhelmed and underqualified USCG Inspection Officer (IO) personnel cited by the Office of Inspector General (OIG) Report to Congress dated May 19th 2008. (Appendix III) In which the USCG Headquarters was found to have a backlog of more than 4,000 investigations in November 2006, with only one (1) person assigned to the review and closure process. The (OIG) Report also disclosed deficiencies in USCG personnel relative to qualification for Marine Casualty Investigating Officer Doctrine, and their decreasing experience.

As stated in the Toledo Express prefacing section *"This companion book pulls back a veil to provide a measure of public exposure to unspoken facts (about Fitzgerald) and regulatory agency oversight."*

While the veil was only partly withdrawn to give initial (un-detailed) visibility to the successful CRA research areas, it does *not* reflect the many other exploratory pathways that declined to yield information, in the search for truth and court resolution.

Due to space limitations, considerable detailed references were omitted from the text, but are *held by CRA* in the form of audio and video recordings with documentary evidence for *courtroom rehearing* support as appropriate, and if called upon to provide prima facie evidence and expert witness testimony in the future.

May the good Lord give all great Lakes mariners kinder November Gitche Gumee sailing conditions, and may your Lakers safely carry you and your essential cargoes wherever you may be called upon to voyage.

Raymond Ramsay   March 24th, 2009

- 17.2 -
SUMMATION

Re: Post-Mortem Review

In preface to this companion book, the Author stated that it would present a new review of hitherto unspoken circumstances, that could have contributed to the demise of S.S. Edmund Fitzgerald.

The book preparation did enter into some (1950's) sensitive elements of Seaway-sized Laker design, construction, operation, safety regulation and November Gitchee Gumee storm weather conditions...all of which had influence on the hierarchical structuring of most-probable cause scenarios attributable to the casualty.

Indeed, this was a challenging undertaking, especially after shortfalls were discovered in the theoretical and empirical discovery stage, some of which will remain contentious (to others) although all were untainted by willful behavior or wrongdoing before and during Great Lakes service.

Owners And Operators

The vessel was a sponsored investment of the Northwestern Mutual Life Insurance Company to provide bulk-cargo carrying services throughout an enlarged lock system of the new (1959) Seaway System. She was <u>not</u> owned by a steel-making industry, but did transport record-breaking ore cargoes for them. Her high powering and efficient propulsion system enabled her to be driven hard and successive Captains Lambert, Newman, Pulcer, and McSorley were each highly-capable ship masters loyally serving the Columbia Transportation Division of the Oglebay Norton Company to whom Fitzgerald was chartered.

Throughout her short 17-year life, it is fair to comment that the officers and crews of the S.S. Edmund Fitzgerald appear to have been carefully selected and well-matched to the vessel's uniquely high performance capabilities and reputation as "Pride of The American Flag." However, the vessel's shortened life-cycle history and sinking still merit explanation at all levels, minus conjecture and biased analysis.

Mission And Design

As with any journey, one should start with mission definition as a prerequisite which, in this case, included Fitzgerald's higher-speed and increased bulk-cargo hauling requirement over specific Great Lakes routes.

As follow-on, a professional American naval architectural company developed conceptual preliminary and contract design specifications and drawings for review and approval by the owner, the regulatory United States Coast Guard (USCG), and the American Bureau of Shipping (ABS). The basic specifications on which the design was predicated were:

- The largest size permitted to transit the Seaway lock system.
- Service speed of 16.3 mph
- Fuel to be coal (later oil).
- Propulsion to be geared turbine.

Naval Architecture: Speed And Powering

The hull form lines plan was developed by the Great Lakes Engineering Works (GLEW) shipyard design staff, and self-propulsion model tests were conducted at the Wageningen model basin in the Netherlands.

To optimize hydrodynamic hull form performance relative to water flow characteristics in the region of the single, non-controllable pitch propeller of 19-1/2 feet diameter, studies were, also undertaken at the U.S. Navy's David Taylor Model Basin at Carderock, Maryland under various operating conditions.

Naval Architecture: Hull Structure

This design element had lesser scientific proofing and higher technical risk than the foregoing, and was heavily dependent on historical empiricism, extrapolation, and past experience with earlier Laker design and construction. The prevailing USCG Load Line Regulations and ABS criteria did not <u>directly</u> apply to the new 729-foot vessel having an increased slenderness (stiffness) ratio exceeding L/D=14 (actual 18.2), and specific welding and inspection requirements for almost <u>all-welded</u> hull structures fabricated for the first time in modular form at the GLEW shipyard.

Also, during the period (thru 1973) when reduced freeboard (deeper draft) was authorized to increase cargo-carrying capacity by about 4,000 tons (15%), no additional hull structural reinforcement was designed or installed. Further, the (5/16th inch thick) steel hatch covers and coamings were not increased in strength to withstand increased water pressure from higher boarding seas.

The 519-feet long cargo hold was compartmented by three (3) non-watertight screen bulkheads, with spar deck loading and unloading access for cargo through twenty-one (21) hatch openings. Each of which created a deck opening measuring 48 feet x 11 feet, and had (1428) Kestner-clamped steel covers to preserve watertightness and hull reserve buoyancy.

While this cargo-handling arrangement was compatible with existing terminal facility characteristics, the deck openings did eliminate about thirty percent (30%) of the continuous spar deck structural plating from the hull girder extreme fiber at the greatest distance from the vessel's neutral axis, and extended to sixty-four percent (64%) of the overall deck width in twenty-one locations. These structural discontinuities are considered to have negatively affected hull strength with vulnerability to fatiguing, springing, bending and torsional effects.

As with many bulk-cargo carriers, the Fitzgerald's spar deck underside was framed with numerous (difficult to weld and inspect) longitudinal and transverse members. Inspection records revealed that their end-connections were repeatedly susceptible to localized structural fatigue cracking, through combined stressing by dynamic torsional, vertical and lateral forces while underway.

The welding procedures and production quality control for standard and higher-strength shipbuilding steel, contributed to these failures when building-berth settling, material expansion and contraction, and dimensional tolerance variations affected (forced) fabrication alignments for required welded joint fit-up throughout the vessel.

And, in October 1976, <u>the American Society for Testing Materials (ASTM) cited a need for proper stress relief</u> of hull structural least-cost, high-production working conditions.

In the 1950's era, photo-elastic iconic modeling and finite element analysis were <u>un</u>available to Laker designers, who applied their personal experience and judgment. The Author has always considered the stress-raising area, at the hull structure's spar deck and Cellular Double Bottom (CDB) extreme fiber zones as major contributors to bulk-cargo carrier structural vulnerabilities, and to the Fitzgerald's hull fracturing at about Frame No. 178 (approximately 0.22L from the stern) under Lake Superior storm conditions.

Elsewhere there is considerable empirical evidence supportive of "long-ship" losses experienced by early supertankers and bulk-cargo vessels when designs had slenderness (stiffness) ratios greater than $L/D=14$, with fractures at approximately 0.25L from the stern...which were later minimized through dedicated Research, Development, Test and Evaluation (RDT&E) principles, in seeking new technical approaches and "build and bust" developments throughout international maritime communities.

In the course of reading official reports, non-eyewitness accounts, and having personal contacts with regulatory, technical, shipyard production and mariner personnel, a framework of credible contributory evidence was formed by Casualty Research Associates (CRA) upon which an objective prioritized technical approach to Fitzgerald's loss could be developed.

While the Author's professional naval architect background in the private and government maritime sectors (including GLEW shipyard involvement with the S.S. Edmund Fitzgerald) does have strong technical interest, the humanitarian conditions for mariner crew members is an intrinsic part of expressed viewpoints.

Casualty Considerations

The primary consideration gives credence to the S.S. Edmund Fitzgerald as the first "beyond the state of the art" design challenge for a large and fast Laker specifically designed and built using modular construction methodology heavily dependent on a mainly welded (versus riveted) hull fabrication practices.

However, the Author's technical involvement made discoveries of concern that included an absence of Research, Development, Testing and Evaluation (RDT&E) principles as prerequisites for design, production, training and maintenance execution. A situation not unique to the GLEW and other Great Lakes shipyard practices.

In section 15 Lemma 8, the Author has offered rationale considered germane to Fitzgerald's initial spar deck fracturing at the mid-length of Cargo Hold No. 3 (0.25L). The preponderance of historical evidence reveals that the onset of this structural failure, would have occurred under high boarding sea hydrostatic and hydrodynamic forces and would be dependent on a multiplicity of conditions coincident with dynamic ship motions.

In sequential combination, there appears to be a number of Failure Mode and Effect Analysis (FMEA) technical elements that are considered attributable to Fitzgerald's loss, and accountable to the experience of others. Primary FMEA elements which were considered accountable to designer and regulatory bodies included, but were not limited to:

- Origination of (1950's) hull strength weaknesses in the design phase when extrapolating beyond the regulatory limits of United

States Coast Guard (USCG) Load Line Regulations, and exceeding the American Bureau of Shipping (ABS) criteria for lesser Laker vessels...without investment in RDT&E principles.

- Lack of hull structural reinforcement retrofitting for compatibility with Load Line Regulation Amendment (46 CFR 45) authorizing freeboard reductions (deeper draft) and enabling a cargo deadweight overload of about 4,000 tons per trip.

- Lack of steel hatch cover and coaming retrofitting of reinforcements for structural compatibility with freeboard reductions that facilitated deeper immersion from boarding seas. The hatch cover system exposure to increased hydrostatic and hydrodynamic water loadings almost doubled 4 foot waterhead loading weathertightness testing requirements for the original design as stipulated by 46 CFR 45.145.

- Unpredictable buckling failure of No. 21 Cargo Hatch (5/16th inch thick steel) cover and coaming, and possibly unseen others below the inverted hull section. The pathway of an abnormal (overtaking) Constructive Interference Wave system boarding from astern and engulfing the starboard quarter, would have introduced a severe asymmetric loading component that cyclically acted with rotational and contra-rotational effect on the storm-tossed vessel.

These events of short duration would have incurred:
- Uncontrollable flooding of the void Cargo Hold No. 3 space above the stowed high-density taconite cargo (with a time lapse of 14 seconds or less) subsequent to hatch cover collapse.
- Critical longitudinal hull loading imbalance caused by a "stern-heavy" condition conducive to catastrophic hull girder failure.
- A rolling motion degenerating to an unrecoverable permanent listing condition, coupled with increased and irreversible sinkage of a plunging stern (Section 15-Lemmas 6, 7 and 8), coincident

with rapid inundation by an estimated 4,431 tons of added lake water weight...in about 14 seconds.

- Generation of fatal multi-directional spar deck stressing overloads induced by (downward) bow motion pitching, slamming, yawing and rotational flexing in a stern-heavy trimmed condition. The Author considers such an overwhelming stressing field would have been capable of causing spar deck fracturing at about the mid-length of Cargo Hold No. 3 (Frame 178), with propagation joining to hull side-shell separation in way of No. 7 Ballast Tank located at the stern starboard quarter.

- Rapid further propagation would have been experienced with torsional tear-away of the "hinging-downward" stern section, as the vessel's forward speed and motions decayed from stern drogue effects during the final sinking evolution.

- Upon separation, the stern section's geometric hull form, buoyancy and weight distribution, would have contributed to hydrostatic instability and roll-over capsizing at an early stage, before sinking to an inverted position at a depth of 530 feet...without any conclusive evidence of shoaling damage recorded on CURV 111 surveying videotapes, although (some) other private investigators believe otherwise.

Subsystem Discussion

The Toledo Express insight appears to have served its search-for-truth purpose by exposing the S.S. Edmund Fitzgerald's hull structural design inadequacies; clarifying shoaling premises; illumination of maintenance and repair negligence; and providing a sound basis for exoneration of the Fitzgerald's officers and crew members. Evidentiary justification is available for the seeking of a rehearing in the U.S. Department of Justice...for the benefit of bereaved laker families. However, CRA volunteer work on this noble cause is still seeking baseline information for the following items.

Radar Systems

Radar system maintenance history is sought to determine:
- If necessary upkeep was deferred since this was (supposedly) Fitzgerald's last trip before end of season shipyard layup...thereby possibly explaining en-route claims of inoperability.
- If one or both radar range antenna systems became inoperable when reported as "...between 1610-1615 hrs. when about three to five miles East of Caribou Island, its closest point of approach to the island..." In view of contradictory and inconsistent navigational testimony at the hearing, CRA considers it of importance to independently ascertain and verify the duration and closeness of Fitzgerald's variable course proximities to the Canadian coastline littoral zone.
- It needs to be determined why the Fitzgerald missed giving required weather reports scheduled for 1300 and 1900 hours on November 10th 1975. Reports were never received (or were never transmitted), especially under severe storm conditions, <u>when others would want their reports.</u>

Could it be:
- Loss of electrical power caused by fractured tunnel conduit or inoperable battery-powered units in the pilothouse?
- Weather instrumentation failure under severe ambient storm conditions, thereby impeding full data measurement?
- Pilothouse crew incapacitation?
- Other?

Damaged Vents

The CRA technical review of flooding consequences which could result from <u>either the loss of two eight-inch diameter tunnel</u> or two <u>ballast tank vents,</u> is in agreement with USCG findings that the events would not be serious enough to cause the loss of the vessel…although the ingress of off-center added water weight would be contributory to a listing condition affecting ship handling and boarding sea occurrences.

The flooding effects from downed eight-inch diameter tunnel vent openings in the spar deck, caused by heavy seas bringing aboard U.F.O. (Unidentified Floating Object) were also addressed in the Author's book "For Whom The Bells Toll," and is given similar credibility as the USCG findings.

Speed Reductions

The Fitzgerald speed variations incurred tantalizing prognostications (to some) since slowing down was contrary to Captain McSorley's reputation as an experienced mariner, and as a "Company-Man" dedicated to safe and speedy vessel operations having compatibility with Fitzgerald's powerful propulsion machinery capabilities.

However, under extant abnormal November 10th storm conditions, with inoperable radar, and a poorly-maintained damaged flexing hull, it is CRA's opinion that he was exercising good seamanship and technical judgment by seeking to reduce the frequency and headings for the minimizing of (a) Bow wave slamming encounters and in the interest of (b) Reducing damaging hull vibration and further structural looseness and (c) Reducing the single-screw (19-1/2 feet diameter) propeller rotational speed in an effort to seek a speed range outside the natural frequency of the hull to avoid sympathetic vibratory excitation..

The Author sincerely hopes that the Fitzgerald's "Toledo Express" (insider) perspective may serve as a useful companion to the book "For Whom The Bells Toll" which also addressed the British M.V. Derbyshire (ore/bulk/oil carrier) sinking tragedy having design and construction beyond the prevailing Classification Society (Lloyds Register) state of the art.

In truth, commercial shipbuilding cannot prosper on empiricism alone but must be an amalgam of shipbuilding traditional art and rigorous Research, Development, Test and Evaluation (RDT&E).

- 18.0 -
REFERENCES AND RESOURCES

Abbreviations:
    A.B.S. American Bureau of Shipping.
    C.F.R. Code of Federal Regulations.
    IACS International Association of Classification Societies
    L.R. Lloyd's Register
    L.C.A. Lake Carriers Association
    MARAD Maritime Administration
    N.O.A.A. National Oceanic and Atmospheric Administration
    N.W.S. National Weather Service
    N.T.S.B. National Transportation Safety Board
    S.L.S.D.C. St. Lawrence Seaway System Development Corp.
    S.N.A.M.E. Society of Naval Architects and Marine Engineers.
    T.S.B. Transportation Safety Board of Canada.
    U.N.C.T.D. United Nations Council on Trading Development
    U.S. D.O.T. United States Department of Transportation.
    U.S.A.C.O.E. Untied States Army Corps of Engineers.
    U.S.C.G. United States Coast Guard.

Reference Sources:

The following is a representative, but not exhaustive, listing of reference sources used in the book preparation. They did augment personal memory recall which, by the grace of God, was not impaired by "senior citizen moments" of relapse. To any technical reader critical of the author's listing of dated reference sources, they may be assured that this was done with deliberate intent and is appropriate to the merchant ship design and construction of the 1950s era.

    American Meteorological Society May 2006 Hurltquist - NOAA (NWS)
    A Ship Too Far M.V. Derbyshire), Ramwell and Madge, 1992.
    Basic Naval Architecture. K.C. Barnaby, 1954.
    Bently Historical Library - University of Michigan
    Bowling Green University, Great Lakes Historical Collections.
    Congressional Hearing, May 19, 2008 OIG-08-51
    Davie Shipbuilding Co. and Successors, S. Kack, 2000.
    Derbyshire Family Association, D.C. Ramwell, P. Lambert.

Design of Merchant Ships. Schokker, Neuerburg, Vossnack: 1953.
Detroit Historical Society
Donald Hermanson Collection
Dossin Great Lakes Museum Archives
Duluth Shipping News
Fifty Years of Furness-Evans 2002
For Whom The Bells Toll: Ramsay 2006
Fraser Shipyard Archives
Great Lakes Historical Society
Great Lakes Maritime Institute
Great Lakes Maritime Institute, Dossin Museaum: J. Polacsek, 2003.
Great Lakes Pilot Vol. 5 No. 7. 2008-Bad Design, Bad Steel, Brittle Fracture by Droulliard and Lawson.
Great Lakes Shipwreck Historical Society: T. Farnquist, 2004.
Hainault, Paul, 1979 All About The Singing of the Sirens That Sank The Fitz..
Hydrographic Service, Ottawa, Canada.
Jack Deo - Superior View, Marquette, Michigan
Lake Superior Maritime Collections - University of Wisconsin-Superior
Lake Superior Maritime Museum Association - LSMMA
Marine Investigation Reports. TSB Canada
Marine Casualty Report 16732/64216, USDOT/USCG, 1977.
Marine Accident Report Mar 78-3, NTSB, 1978.
Marine Engineering. SNAME, 1976.
Mechanics of Materials. Popov, 1957
Michigan Maritime Museum
Ministry of Geology and Mines Report, Thunder Bay, Canada.
National Research Journal 2001.
NTSB Marine Accident Report Mar-78-3.
Nautical Research Guild
Naval Architect's and Shipbuilder's Pocketbook. Mackrow: 1954.
Oceaneering International. L. Karl: 2004.
Pride of the Inland Sea. B. Beck and C.P. Labadie: 2004
Shipwrecks of the Lakes-Dana T. Bowen.
Ship Design and Construction, SNAME: 1969, 2003.
Ships for Victory: F.C. Lane, 2001.
Ship Construction and Calculations. Nicol: 1937.
SNAME Paper, St. Lawrence River Canal Vessels. Gilmore: 1957.
SNAME Paper, S.S. Edmund Fitzgerald Engine Room Design. Varian, Spooner, 1958.
SNAME Paper, "Recent Research on Dynamic Behavior of Large Great Lakes SNAME Bulk Carriers," Stiansen: 1984.
S.S. Edmund Fitzgerald Mystique and Its Evolution, Murphy: 2001.
Strength of Materials, Timoshenko: 1956
Theoretical Naval Architecture. Attwood and Pengally: 1899-1946.
Toledo Blade, Ohio. Nov. 13, 1975.
The Night The Fitz Went Down. H.E. Bishop & Capt. Dudley J. Parquette: 2000.
U.S. Coast Guard Archives (Richard Sullivan Photos - 1999)
USCG Marine Casualty Report 16732/64216

The Edmund Fitzgerald Hull Failure. Capt. Richard Orgel 2008.
UK High Court of Justice Report of the Reopened Formal Investigation in to the Loss of M.V. Derbyshire Nov. 2000.
USCG Archives (G-IPA-4).
University of Detroit - Mercy - Marine Historical Collections
Wisconsin Marine Historical Society - Milwaukee Public Library
Wisconsin Maritime Museum
Wreck of the Edmund Fitzgerald. F. Stonehouse: 1977.
RINA Paper, "Design and Operation of Bulk Carriers," 2001.
RINA Paper, "An Analytical Assessment of the M.V. Derbyshire Sinking," Faulkner: 2001.
River Rouge Historical Museum, Michigan: D. Swekel, 2002.
Sault Evening News, Sault Ste. Marie, Michigan, Nov. 11, 1975.
Sea Technology, Compass Publications, Volume 35 No. 12, Dec. 1994.
The Edmund Fitzgerald Hull Failure-Orgal 2008.
The Toledo Express: Ramsay 2009

The Final Hour
Painting by Mary C. Demroske

Shares Proposed in Bradley Claims

Appendix I
Cleveland Plain Dealer
June 14, 1960

By J. C. DASCHBACH

Recommendations for sharing of a $1,250,000 settlement fund in the sinking of the freighter Carl D. Bradley were made in a report filed in U.S. District Court late yesterday by Jerome N. Curtis, Cleveland lawyer.

Thirty-three men died in the disaster and two survived.

Curtis was appointed commissioner by Judge Charles J. McNamee to take testimony on the claims and recommend apportionments.

$43,673 for Family Here

Raymond G. Buehler, 58, the chief engineer, was the only crew member from Greater Cleveland. His widow, Mrs. Frances J. Buehler, and their 20-year-old daughter, Bonita Ann, live at 1500 Cordova Avenue, Lakewood. The engineer's mother also lives there.

Curtis set the Buehlers' pro rata share at $43,673.56. Buehler's average earnings were set at $16,408 a year by Curtis and his life expectancy was 16 years.

The recommendations on a pro rata basis range from zero to $73,309.19.

The Bradley sank in a storm 10 miles off Gull Island in Lake Michigan Nov. 18, 1958.

June 28 Is Deadline

Suits totaling more than 16 million dollars were filed against the United States Steel Corp., owner of the ship. On Dec. 5, 1959, a settlement was made whereby U. S. Steel set aside $1,250,000 for all claims. Claimants now have until June 28 to file exceptions to the findings of Curtis. If there are none, Judge McNamee will then review the Curtis report and determine whether it should be approved or modified.

Curtis held hearings in Rogers City and Detroit, Mich., and in Cleveland.

The estate of Roland Bryan, 52, captain of the Bradley, was allotted $10,294.48. His home was in Collingwood, Ont. He was unmarried and his parents were deceased, the report says. However, he made contributions to an invalid sister.

The largest share recommended by Curtis was $73,309.19 for the estate of John F. Fogelsonger, 31, second mate. He is survived by his wife, Mary Fogelsonger, 29, and two children, John F. Jr., 1, and Sheri-Marie, 2 months at the time of the sinking. His net average earnings were $9,980 a year and his life expectancy was set at 38.2 years.

The two survivors of the disaster were Elmer H. Fleming, 44, first mate, and Frank Mays, 29, a deckhand. Curtis recommended $6,239.08 for Fleming and $13,725.98 for Mays. Both complain of grievous after-effects of their hours-long ordeal in the water.

Those who lost their lives, their survivors and the amounts recommended by Curtis for their surviving dependents, with ages as of time of sinking, were:

CARL BARTELL JR., 24, third mate; his widow, Joan Bartell, and one daughter, Carla Sue, 3; $63,638.62.

JOHN L. BAUERS, 30, second assistant engineer; his widow, Alleen Bauers, and two children, Mary J., 3, and Jerry T., 1; $71,749.42.

DOUGLAS BELLMORE, 34, a porter; his widow, Flora Bellmore, three children by a former marriage, Linda Lou, 11, Sharon Ann, 9, and Terry Lee, 6; $27,451.95.

DUANE BERG, 25, a deckhand; his widow, Donna Berg, and one child, Duane M., born after the father's death; $36,496.62.

ALFRED F. BOEHMER, 32, second assistant engineer; his widow, Dolores Boehmer, and two sons, Philip M., 2, and Eric D., 8 months; $71,125.51.

ALVA BUDNICK, 27, deckwatch; his widow, Frances A. Budnick, and three children, Kim, 3, Toni, 2, and Candace, 3 months; $51,472.41.

WILLIAM T. ELLIOTT, 26, repatrman and watchman; his widow, Sandra Elliott, and two children, William T. Jr., 2, and Deborah L., 1; $58,647.38.

CLYDE M. ENOS, 30, stokerman; unmarried; leaves his father, J. Martin Enos, and his mother, who has been an invalid 15 years; $8,110.80.

ERHARDT O. FELAX, 47, stokerman; his widow, Barbara Felax, and two daughters, Linda Sue, 11, and Dona Rae, 7; $52,425.74.

CLELAND E. GAGER, 30, an oiler; his widow, Patricia G. Gager, and three children, Cheryl Rae, 8, Michael E., 6, and Daniel L., 4; $49,263.73.

PAUL GRENGTSKI, 24, a watchman; his widow, Patricia A. Grengtski, and a daughter, Susan Jean, 6 months; $45,233.33.

PAUL HELLER, 45, stokerman; his widow, Adeline Heller, and two children, Mark, 17, and Raye, 12; $39,930.11.

PAUL R. HORN, 31, an oiler; unmarried; leaves his mother, Edna Horn, 56; $8,110.80.

DENNIS M. JOPPICH, 19, a wiper; unmarried; leaves his parents, Mr. and Mrs. William F. Joppich; $10,606.44.

RAYMOND J. KOWALSKI, 31, a wheelsman; his widow, Mavis Kowalski, and four children, Brenda Sue, 8, Michael Gary, 6, Richard Paul, 2, and Mary Jane, 6 months; $57,711.49.

JOSEPH KRAWCZAK, a wheelsman; his widow, Cecilia Krawczak, and six children, Ronald J., 11, Jacinta M., 10, Rose A., 7, Kathryn M., 4, Andrea A., 3, and Jo Lynn, 3 months; $56,151.72.

FLOYD A. MacDOUGALL, 27, assistant repairman; his widow, Genevieve A., and two children, Debra Lynn, 4, and Denise Marie, 6 months; $42,425.74.

DENNIS B. MEREDITH, 25, a deckhand; unmarried; leaves his parents, Mr. and Mrs. George B. Meredith, 61 and 57; $6,862.99.

MELVILLE W. ORR, 35, deckwatch; his widow, Barbara F. Orr, and three children, Susan Kaye, 12, Patricia Ann, 11, and Melvin Gary, 10; $47,728.96.

ALFRED G. PILARSKI, 30, second cook; unmarried; leaves his mother, Sally Pilarski, 57; $8,734.71.

GARY N. PRICE, 21, a deckhand; his widow, Helen A. Price, and a son, Ronald G., 4 months; $43,361.61.

LEO PROMO JR., 21, a wiper; his widow Mary M. Promo, and a son born after the father's death; $30,883.45.

BERNARD J. SCHEFKE, 19, a porter; unmarried; leaves his father and mother, Robert Schefke, 61, and Victoria Schefke, 55; $5,615.17.

KEITH M. SCHULER, 36, third assistant engineer; his widow Marjorie E. Schuler, and three children, Duwayne K., 15, Randall L., 11, and Jane Ann, 9; $63,638.62.

JAMES L. SELKE, 18, a porter; unmarried; leaves his parents, Mr. and Mrs. Alexander Selke; $5,615.17.

GARY L. STRZELECKI, 21, a deckwatch; his widow, Ann S. Strzelecki, and a son, Benjamin W., 9 months; $46,795.10.

EARL TULGETSKE JR., 30, a wheelsman; his widow, Eleanor M. Tulgetske, and four children, Karen Diane, 6, Susan Lynn, 5, Paul Edward, 3, and Leslie Ann, 1; $54,903.90.

EDWARD VALLEE, 49, a conveyorman; his widow, Frances E. Vallee, and two children, Patricia

Appendix II
1975

Fitz owner files liability petition

CLEVELAND (AP)—The owner and operator of the sunken Great Lakes ore carrier Edmund Fitzgerald Monday filed a petition in U. S. District Court here to determine liability for the vessel's sinking.

The Northwest Mutual Life Insurance Co., the Fitzgerald's owner, and the Oglebay-Norton Co. filed the petition to answer a suit filed Nov. 17 on behalf of two of the missing crewmen of the ship.

In a statement issued Monday, Oglebay-Norton said: "The tragic sinking on Nov. 10 of the steamer Edmund Fitzgerald in a violent Lake Superior storm is under investigation by a Coast Guard Board of inquiry. We are working with the Coast Guard in doing everything possible to determine the cause of this disaster. As of this date, the inquiry has not been completed and findings have not been made."

The board of inquiry adjourned until Dec. 10 after eight days of testimony.

The company said its petition "is a necessary legal step to bring all other claims into one Federal District Court so that the legal rights of all parties affected will be determined on the basis of the same facts and law and assure uniform treatment with a minimum of inconvenience and delay. All representatives of the men who were aboard the Fitzgerald will receive notices of the action taken and will have an opportunity to file claims."

John J. Dwyer, president of Oglebay Norton, said, "In the interest of all who sail the Great Lakes, we must do everything possible to determine the cause of the sinking of the Fitzgerald."

"Oglebay-Norton is in close touch with every family involved to make sure that none lacks the immediate financial support it needs," he added.

Board of inquiry chairman Rear Adm. Winford W. Barrow, said when the hearings were adjourned, "The testimony indicated it (the ship) broke up rather suddenly, catastrophically."

He said it appears unlikely the wreckage can be raised from a depth of 530 feet.

Appendix III

U.S. House of Representatives
Committee on Transportation and Infrastructure
Washington, DC 20515

James L. Oberstar
Chairman

John L. Mica
Ranking Republican Member

David Heymsfeld, Chief of Staff
Ward W. McCarragher, Chief Counsel

May 19, 2008

James W. Coon II, Republican Chief of Staff

SUMMARY OF SUBJECT MATTER

TO: Members of the Subcommittee on Coast Guard and Maritime Transportation

FROM: Subcommittee on Coast Guard and Maritime Transportation Staff

SUBJECT: Hearing on "Coast Guard and National Transportation Safety Board Casualty Investigation Program"

PURPOSE OF THE HEARING

On Tuesday, May 20, 2008, at 10:00 a.m., in Room 2167 of the Rayburn House Office Building, the Subcommittee on Coast Guard and Maritime Transportation will meet to receive a report from the Department of Homeland Security's Office of the Inspector General ("OIG") entitled "United States Coast Guard's Management of the Marine Casualty Investigation Program" (OIG-08-51, May 2008). The Subcommittee will also receive testimony from the National Transportation Safety Board ("NTSB") and the Coast Guard regarding the issue of which agency should exercise primacy in the conduct of marine casualty investigations.

BACKGROUND

The investigation of accidents (also know as "casualties") -- whether they involve ships, planes, trains, trucks or automobiles – provides a foundation for Congress and the executive branch agencies to review and amend transportation safety legislation and regulation. Without a thorough investigation into the causes of accidents through the development of comprehensive information on all aspects of the accident, including all potential causal factors, it is difficult if not impossible to develop legislation or regulations that can effectively prevent future accidents.

Review of Marine Casualty Investigation Program – U.S. Coast Guard

Statutes

The casualty investigation procedure codified in Chapter 63 of Title 46, United States Code, has its origins in public law number 622, which reorganized the Bureau of Marine Inspection and Navigation ("BMIN"), a precursor service eventually folded into the modern day Coast Guard. Adopted in 1936, P.L. 74-622 established Marine Casualty Investigation Boards – to be comprised of a chairman representing the Department of Justice, and two additional members, one member representing the BMIN and one member representing the Coast Guard – to investigate serious casualties involving loss of life. For casualties that did not result in loss of life, a Marine Board made up of two traveling inspectors and one supervising inspector of the BMIN was to be appointed by the Secretary of Commerce.

These Boards were abolished by Reorganization Plan No. 3 of 1946, which permanently transferred the BMIN from the U.S. Department of Treasury to the U.S. Coast Guard. However, the tradition of assembling formal panels to examine marine accidents continues in current practice.

Thus, today, Section 6301 of title 46 requires the Coast Guard to investigate marine casualties to determine the cause of the casualty, including the cause of any death, and to determine whether:

- there is "misconduct, incompetence, negligence, unskillfullness, or willful violation of law committed by any licensed individual;"
- "misconduct, incompetence, negligence, unskillfullness, or willful violation of law committed by any person, including any officer, employee, or member of the Coast Guard, contributed to the cause of the casualty or death involved in the casualty;"
- "there is evidence of an act subjecting the offender to a civil penalty;"
- "there is evidence of a criminal act" that should be referred to appropriate authorities for prosecution; and
- "there is a need for new laws or regulations, or amendment or repeal of existing laws or regulations to prevent the recurrence of the casualty". 46 U.S.C. 6301.

Online Posting of Casualty Reports Required

Section 442 of the Maritime Transportation Security Act of 2002 (P.L. 107-295) amended chapter 61 of title 46, United States Code, to require the Coast Guard to make available in electronic format all casualty reports (i.e., to post them online). At the present time, the Coast Guard posts on-line the information recorded in its Marine Information Safety and Law Enforcement ("MISLE") database. In many cases, the information in MISLE does not provide specific information regarding the cause of a casualty, or the recommendations (if any) developed by the investigator to prevent future casualties.

A recent example of a failure to post complete casualty information online involves the tragic death of a crewmember of the inspected Sailing Vessel (S/V) ALABAMA. On July 14, 2006, Benjamin Sutherland, an 18-year-old crewmember of the S/V ALABAMA, fell to his death while trying to cross between the two masts of the vessel on the "spring stay" – a taught wire cable stretched between the foremast and the mainmast. The following data is posted on the Coast Guard's website regarding that casualty: "A crew member of the Schooner ALABAMA accidently fell from the mast rigging and suffered fatal injuries. Vessel was approximately one hour into a scheduled day trip on Vineyard Sound and was carrying 45 passengers. Weather was calm with reported wave height of 1-2 ft, and winds were at 15 knots in a NW direction." No other information is publicly available.

However, two newspapers, *The Martha's Vineyard Times* and the *Vineyard Gazette*, submitted a Freedom of Information Act ("FOIA") request for the Coast Guard's full casualty investigation report on the ALABAMA and received considerably more information than was made available online. Subcommittee staff requested and received a copy of the information provided to the newspapers. While the report contains no evidence of violations of statute or regulations, there were two important safety recommendations contained in the report aimed at preventing such tragedies in the future, including a recommendation for the development of a regulation regarding the use of safety harnesses onboard similar sailing vessels, and a recommendation regarding the development of safety policies by the owners of such passenger vessels. In addition, the complete report includes the narrative report compiled by the Coast Guard investigator along with written statements by witnesses.

Furthermore, unlike other safety agencies, the Coast Guard does not post all marine casualty safety recommendations on the Internet or conduct follow-up assessments to ensure that the recommendations have been implemented.

Regulations

Regulations (46 CFR Part 4) provide that the Coast Guard's investigation of a marine casualty "will determine as closely as possible:
1) The cause of the accident (emphasis added);
2) Whether there is evidence that any failure of material (either physical or design) was involved or contributed to the casualty, so that proper recommendations for the prevention of the recurrence of similar casualties may be made;
3) Whether there is evidence that any act of misconduct, inattention to duty, negligence or willful violation of the law on the part of any licensed or certificated person contributed to the casualty, so that appropriate proceedings against the license or certificate of such person may be recommended and taken under 46 U.S.C. 6301;
4) Whether there is evidence that any Coast Guard personnel or any representative or employee of any other government agency or any other person caused or contributed to the cause of the casualty; or,
5) Whether the accident shall be further investigated by a Marine Board of Investigation in accordance with regulations in subpart 4.09.[1]

Section 4.07-10 of the regulations requires the investigating officer to submit a report to the Commandant as follows –

> (a) At the conclusion of the investigation the investigating officer shall submit to the Commandant via the Officer in Charge, Marine

---

[1] 46 CFR 4.07-1.

Inspection, and the District Commander, a full and complete report of the facts as determined by his investigation, together with his opinions and recommendations in the premises. The Officer in Charge, Marine Inspection, and the District Commander shall forward the investigating officer's report to the Commandant with an endorsement stating:
1) Approval or otherwise of the findings of fact, conclusions and recommendations;
2) Any action taken with respect to the recommendations;
3) Whether or not any action has been or will be taken under part 5 of this subchapter to suspend or revoke licenses or certificates; and,
4) Whether or not violations of laws or regulations relating to vessels have been reported on Form CG-2636, report of violation of navigation laws.[2]

Policy Letters/Marine Safety Manual

In addition to statute and regulation, the Coast Guard provides guidance on marine casualty investigations through its Marine Safety Manual and Policy Letters. Chapter 5 of the Marine Safety Manual, entitled "Levels of Effort and Types of Investigations", was recently updated (April 24, 2008) to incorporate guidance from a series of Policy Letters dating back to the mid-1990s. The Chapter covers such issues as "Preliminary Investigation", "Data Collection", and "Informal" and "Formal" Investigations.

The Chapter states that "Preliminary Investigations" are used to determine the seriousness of a casualty or pollution incident and to determine whether further investigation or notification of other agencies is required.

"Data Collection" is required for all reportable marine casualties not assigned to Informal or Formal Investigations. Thus, the Chapter notes that "Data collection is the minimum level of investigation required when there will be no analysis, conclusions, or recommendations stemming from an investigation." Data collection is "intended to document the facts surrounding an incident for the public record and must meet the investigative obligations outlined in 46 U.S.C. 6301" (emphasis added). Data collection does not, however, "decide ... the cause of the casualty ..." as required by Section 6301.

"Informal Investigations" are conducted when there is: a death; serious injury; loss of an uninspected vessel of less than 500 gross tons; loss of a barge of more than 100 gross tons on inland waters; property damage in excess of $100,000 but less than $1,000,000; a collision or allision resulting in property damage exceeding $25,000, loss of propulsion or steering affecting an inspected U.S. vessel, a foreign vessel, or uninspected U.S. vessel of 100 gross tons on U.S. navigable waters; failure of Coast Guard approved equipment; a medium discharge of oil or hazardous substance; a commercial diving casualty; or a recreational diving casualty. Informal investigations are usually carried out by one Investigating Officer ("IO") in conjunction with other staff.

---

[2] 46 CFR 4.07-10.

"Formal Investigations" are conducted when there is: two or more deaths; two or more seriously disabling injuries or six or more injuries which result in fractured bones, loss of limbs, severe hemorrhaging, severe muscle, nerve, tendon or internal organ damage or hospitalization for more than 48 hours within five days of the injury; loss of an inspected vessel or loss of an uninspected vessel of 500 gross tons or more; property damage exceeding $1,000,000; or a major discharge of oil or release of hazardous cargoes. Formal Investigations are usually conducted by a "Marine Board" convened by the Commandant and comprised by three or more members.

The Coast Guard has conducted few three-person Marine Boards of Investigation in the last few years. In this decade, only one Marine Board of Investigation has been completed (the F/V ARCTIC ROSE). There is an ongoing formal investigation into the recent sinking of the F/V ALASKA RANGER. In the 1990s, the Coast Guard conducted 12 Marine Boards, while in the 1980s, 18 Marine Boards were conducted.

Qualifications for Coast Guard Marine Casualty Investigators ("IOs")

Concurrent with the issuance of the revised Marine Safety Manual, the Coast Guard issued a message (known as an ALCOAST) to all Coast Guard personnel regarding "Marine Casualty Investigating Officer Doctrine" that outlines the current qualifications required of Marine Casualty Investigators. Significantly, the message admits that, "there has been an overall decrease in the experience of Coast Guard Marine Casualty Investigators" and that "in an effort to strengthen the Marine Casualty Investigation Program, the Commandant is developing an action plan that will ensure IO billets are staffed with a corps of well trained, certified and experienced Marine Casualty Investigating Officers."

The message outlines the specific steps that an individual must complete to become a Marine Casualty Investigator. Specifically, to become an IO, a person must attend the basic investigating officers training course at the Coast Guard's training center in Yorktown, Virginia. The trainee must then complete a number of performance qualification standards – which are individual skill areas that are learned through on-the-job training, including preparing for investigation, initiating an investigation, generating an incident timeline, conducting causal analysis, conducting human error analysis, drawing and recording conclusions, developing safety recommendations/alerts, and recommending enforcement action. The person must then be examined by a Qualification Board consisting of personnel that are already qualified as Marine Casualty Investigators. Additionally, to be considered certified as a Marine Casualty Investigator, the IO must be assigned to an operational billet as a Marine Casualty Investigator and must be designated in writing as an IO by the cognizant Officer in Charge Marine Inspection.

Importantly, the ALCOAST also appears to presage issues that are addressed in the OIG's report on the Coast Guard's Marine Casualty Program when it states, "If your unit lacks the appropriate certified personnel to conduct a marine casualty investigation, then you shall seek assistance outside of your unit. The Coast Guard is conducting a study of the status of IO qualifications, including personnel currently assigned to IO billets and those with IO certifications not assigned to IO billets."

Report of the Department of Homeland Security Inspector General

In December 2005, the Committee on Transportation and Infrastructure and the Committee on Commerce, Science and Transportation of the Senate requested the OIG "to conduct a study of the Coast Guard's marine casualty investigation program and report to the Committees the finding and recommendations."

The Committees were particularly interested in an examination of "the extent to which marine casualty investigations and reports result in information and recommendations that prevent similar casualties; minimize the effect of similar casualties, given that it has occurred; and maximize lives saved in similar casualties given that the vessel has become uninhabitable."

To promote safety for all who work or travel on the water and to protect the marine environment, the Committees asked that the study and report specifically include an examination of the following issues:

- adequacy of resources devoted to marine casualty investigations considering caseload and duty assignment practices;
- training and experience of marine casualty investigators;
- investigation standards and methods, including a comparison of the formal and informal investigation processes;
- use of best investigation practices considering transportation investigation practices used by other Federal agencies and foreign governments, including British Marine Accident Investigation Branch programs;
- usefulness of the marine casualty database for marine casualty prevention programs;
- the extent to which marine casualty data and information have been used to improve the survivability and habitability of vessels involved in marine casualties;
- any changes to current statutes that would clarify Coast Guard responsibilities for marine casualty investigations and report; and
- the extent to which the Coast Guard has reduced the frequency of formal investigations, or changed the types of incidents for which it has carried out a formal investigation process, in the past five years.

Summary of the Report

The Inspector General's report, entitled "United States Coast Guard's Management of the Marine Casualty Investigation Program", finds that the Coast Guard's marine casualty investigation program is "hindered by unqualified personnel conducting marine casualty investigations; investigations that are conducted at inappropriate levels, and ineffective management of a substantial backlog of investigations needing review and closure."

The Inspector General's report covers the period from January 1, 2003, through October 31, 2006. During this period, the Coast Guard "opened" 15,327 investigations but conducted only 13 formal investigations. As noted above, only one three-person Marine Board of Investigation was conducted during that period.

The OIG found that many of the casualty investigations were not conducted at the level of scope (i.e., formal, informal, data collection) that was appropriate to the circumstances of the casualty under the Coast Guard's own policies. The report identifies more than 1,200 casualties that should have been investigated at a higher level than the level at which they were investigated. Specifically, 134 casualties were examined that should have been investigated at the "formal" level including 55 casualties where only data was collected; 952 casualties that should have been investigated at the "informal" level but for which only data was collected; and, 169 casualties that should have been investigated at the "data collection level or higher but were not."

Some of the "downgrading" was due to a post-9/11 directive that allowed casualty investigations to be investigated at lower levels. However, despite the fact that the "9/11 downgrade directive" was cancelled in 2002, not all units have subsequently conducted investigations in accordance with the directive that replaced the "downgrade directive" (G-MOA Policy Letter 2-02), resulting in a number of casualties that were not investigated at the level required by policy given the nature of the accidents involved.

The OIG also found that a significant number of individuals who are not qualified under Coast Guard standards as casualty investigators are nonetheless assigned to such positions. While conducting site visits, the auditors examined a sample of individuals assigned as investigating officers and found that 68 percent (15 of 22) of the marine casualty investigators did not meet qualification standards. Five of these individuals had not even completed the "basic course" required for all investigators. While this was an admittedly small sample, the Coast Guard did not dispute the results, stating "that the results reflect the qualifications problem facing the marine casualty investigation program nation-wide."

Further, the OIG found that in 2007 the Coast Guard had significantly modified the prerequisites for becoming a casualty investigator by changing the "requirement of a Hull or Machinery and Small Vessel Inspector". The OIG observed that, "When investigators do not have the experience or ability to determine that a hull failure or loss of propulsion are possible causes of a marine casualty, they may not be able to issue the appropriate safety alerts or recommendations to possibly prevent or minimize the effect of similar casualties in the future."

The OIG found that the development within the Coast Guard of qualified casualty investigators is hampered by the following factors:

> "The Coast Guard has not effectively managed and controlled aspects of the marine casualty investigation program to ensure that it obtains and develops qualified investigators;"
> "The Coast Guard has not established a clear and desirable career path for investigator, which can further impede recruitment efforts;" and,
> "Additionally, according to Coast Guard personnel, tour of duty rotations hinder investigators in acquiring the experience needed for career development."

The OIG notes that "In contrast, civilian marine casualty investigators are not subject to the three-year tour of duty rotation standard." Nonetheless, of the 22 marine casualty investigators reviewed by the OIG, only one was a civilian. In 2007, the Coast Guard reported that six civilians are serving as full time marine casualty investigators.

The OIG's report also observes that there are previous reports – including one by the Coast Guard's Research and Development Center conducted in 1994 and one by a Coast Guard Quality Action Team conducted in 1995 – that identified problems with the Coast Guard's efforts to increase the numbers and qualifications of marine casualty investigators.

Finally, the report notes that there is a tremendous backlog of casualty investigations that have not been reviewed or closed and a number of instances in which data collected on an accident were incorrectly entered into the Coast Guard MISLE database. In November 2006, Coast Guard headquarters had a backlog of more than 4,000 investigations of which almost 2,500 (58 percent) had been open and awaiting review and closure for more than six months. Coast Guard headquarters reviews and closes investigations, but only one person was assigned to this process. To reduce this backlog, on September 29, 2006, the Coast Guard closed almost 4,000 investigations that it deemed to be "low risk", including 194 informal investigations and one formal investigation. It is the opinion of the OIG that, "some investigations merited reviews because they involved serious incidents requiring causal analysis" and that "enforcement action also may have resulted from these investigations."

Because so many casualty investigations were closed "en mass", there was no opportunity to "identify errors input to the MISLE database." The Inspector General tested 145 marine casualty investigations and found that 30 percent contained at least one MISLE data error. However, it is unlikely that anyone will review the hundreds of cases that were closed without review and, as a result, the data in those cases will always be suspect. Further, the OIG observed that, although MISLE is designed to "support trend analysis and studies that may result in recommendations and safety alerts", the information in the system is unreliable because of the high error rate.

The Inspector General makes eight recommendations, seven of which have been acted upon by the Coast Guard. The OIG is leaving four of these actions open until details and documentation is provided on actions taken so that the OIG can determine whether they adequately address the findings. The recommendations are listed below.

- Develop and implement a plan to increase the number of qualified marine casualty investigators, including hiring civilian marine casualty investigators, and improving the career path for marine casualty investigators.
- Evaluate re-instituting the four-year tour of duty for active duty marine casualty investigators and ensure that they complete the entire tour of duty as a marine casualty investigator.
- Develop and implement a plan to ensure attendance at the basic and advanced courses for those qualified to attend.
- Revise the August 2007 marine casualty investigation qualification standard to include the prequalification of Hull or Machinery, and Small Vessel Inspectors.
- Implement quality controls to ensure that marine casualty investigations are conducted at the recommended levels, consistent information is gathered, and causal factors are determined when appropriate.
- Review and revise the criteria for the levels of marine casualty investigations, make any appropriate changes to reduce or eliminate conflicting interpretations, and ensure criteria are consistently applied throughout the Coast Guard.
- Finalize and issue the Marine Safety Manual.

➢ Reorganize the headquarters review and closure process to include sufficient staff responsible for reviewing and closing marine casualty investigations, and ensure that the review and closure process is completed in a timely and effective manner.

NATIONAL TRANSPORTATION SAFETY BOARD ("NTSB") REQUEST FOR PRIMACY

The NTSB and the Coast Guard currently share responsibility for the investigation of marine casualties, with the NTSB taking the lead on some major casualties. Recent examples include the investigation of the grounding of the EMPRESS OF THE NORTH and the allision of the M/V COSCO BUSAN with the San Francisco Bay Bridge.

In its draft reauthorization bill, the NTSB proposes to assume "the right to elect lead or primary status in a marine investigation." The NTSB asserts that, "This recommendation is not intended to serve as an expansion of authority by the Board, but to provide the necessary authority if at any time in the immediate aftermath of a marine casualty there is a disagreement between the Board and the Coast Guard created by a disagreement over interpretation of the regulations they have jointly issued; it would thus permit the Board to elect primacy and speed the immediate and urgent investigative process along without confusion over which agency has lead status."

In addition, the Board proposes a new section for "Maritime accident investigation" that in large measure parallels the Board's authority in aviation accidents, and gives the Coast Guard party status in an investigation in the same manner that the Federal Aviation Administration ("FAA") has party status in aviation casualty investigations.

NTSB and Coast Guard Approaches to Investigations

While having similar responsibilities regarding investigation of casualties, the Board and the Coast Guard often approach an investigation with different processes and different objectives. The Board's primary responsibility is to determine the proximate cause of an accident. While responsible for determining proximate cause, the Coast Guard is also charged with determining whether any violations of statute or regulation occurred in conjunction with the accident. At times, this law enforcement function appears to sometimes conflicts with the Coast Guard's search for causal factors.

In addition, the Board is very careful to secure the scene of a casualty and protect all potential evidence. This approach ensures that valuable information is not lost during the early stages of an investigation. In the recent case of the investigation of the COSCO BUSAN (which allided with the San Francisco Bay Bridge in November 2007), investigators from the Board who responded to the incident found that certain important navigational equipment was not only not secured by the Coast Guard, it had not even been identified by Coast Guard investigators (whom the OIG later learned did not meet the Coast Guard's own qualifications for casualty investigators).

When examining an accident, the Board brings together all interested parties, including the Coast Guard, to examine all available evidence. The Board also carefully controls the release of information regarding accident investigations to ensure that a single message is being presented.

PREVIOUS COMMITTEE ACTION

The Subcommittee held a hearing in April 2007, on "Commercial Fishing Vessel Safety" and in August 2007, on "The Challenges Facing the Coast Guard's Marine Safety Program". In November 2007, the Subcommittee conducted a field hearing in San Francisco on the allision of the COSCO BUSAN with the San Francisco Bay Bridge. In April 2008, the Subcommittee held a follow-up hearing on the COSCO BUSAN during which the Department of Homeland Security, Office of Inspector General, testified regarding its report on the "Allision of the M/V COSCO BUSAN with the San Francisco-Oakland Bay Bridge". Each of these hearings examined the Coast Guard's marine safety program, including the casualty investigation mission.

WITNESSES

The Honorable Anne Richards
Assistant Inspector General
Department of Homeland Security

Ms. Kathryn Higgins
Board Member
National Transportation Safety Board

Rear Admiral James Watson, IV
Director of Prevention Policy for Marine Safety, Security, and Stewardship
U.S. Coast Guard

Final resting place of the S.S. Edmund Fitzgerald's bell. A Memorial to the lost mariners at the Shipwreck Museum, Whitefish Point, Michigan.

Image Coutesty of G.L.S.R.H.S.